Wellfleet Tales II

Confessions of a "Wash-Ashore"

Keeping the memories alive

By

Rick Cochran

Rick Cochran

Sharon/Bunkie,
Thank you for your contributions to the tales. Hope you enjoy!
Warm Wishes,
Rick

Wellfleet Tales II

Confessions of a "Wash-Ashore"

Remembering special people, places and times.

Richard Cochran
Bound Brook Isle Publishing
2016

Cover Photo
By
Rick Cochran

ISBN – 13: **978-1530867097**

Contents

Introduction	1
Wellfleet Memories – or – "Sorry I asked"	4

Wellfleet in the Old Days

How We Got To Wellfleet – Left - and Came Back	6
A Perfect Day at the Beaches	9
Mayo Beach on the Bay	11
The Ponds	14
The Back-Shore	19
Our View – Target Ship – Great Blackout	22
Names & Nicknames	25
Sometimes It Hurts To Be A Paine!	26
Wellfleet Politics	27
Charlie Bean	28
Tony's Barbershop	30

Crime & Punishment

The Wellfleet PD	33
Law & Order at the Pier or Don't *** With Charlie	36
The Halloween Prank	40
Wellfleet Outlaws – Kid Costa & Bonnie and Clyde	43

Family - Summer Friends - Wellfleet Activities

Nana	46
Tom Kane Spins Another Dick Cochran Yarn	52
So – How Good Was He?	55
Measure Twice – Cut Once	58
My Paper Route – The Trailer Park – Chipper	64
Cousins and Guests	67
My Other Father	71
Celebrities	74
"We'll Never Catch'em Now"	79
The Weintraubs	82
Boy Scouts and Girl Scouts	86
Wellfleet High School Activities	94

Wellfleet Elementary Teachers

Mrs. Hilda Fleming	97
Mrs. Edith Atwood	98
Mrs. Adah Morton (Dickey)	100
Mrs. Mary Peters	103
Don't Fool with Mrs. Snow	104
Forty Years with Mr. Bacon	105
Mr. Harry Ryder	107
Martha Porch – Old School Classic	110
The Torch Is Passed	113

Photo Essays

The Old Pier and The New Marina	117
Mayo Beach and Chequesset Inn	123
The Railroad Trestle and Oyster Shacks	127
4th of July	130
Wellfleet Churches	134
Wellfleet Baseball	137
Wellfleet Consolidated School Classes	139
Wellfleet Dance Studio	160
Fini	167

Introduction

Wash-ashore- A non-native to a coastal or island community, a subject of suspicion. *Example – He may be married to a native Cape Codder, but he's a wash-ashore.*

Wellfleet Tales II, like the original *Wellfleet Tales*, is a series of stand-alone stories organized thematically and roughly chronologically. Of course, that's a little like when fumble-mouthed baseball manager Casey Stengel, told his team, to line up "alphabetically by height."

One change in this book is the inclusion of photo essays that rely more on pictures than text. The book includes some historical information, and refers to a number of people who were important in the life of the town, or at least important in my life. However, it's not a history; my first goal is to attempt to entertain the reader.

My father, mother and sister Nancy came to Provincetown before I was born, moved to Wellfleet a year later and left the Cape after six years with my sister Judy added, and without a clue that I would someday join them. So the tales from Wellfleet have two parts: the ones passed down to me from before I was born, and the stories that I lived after we moved back in 1952 when I was four years old.

Most of the family stories are about my father, although my mother appears frequently. I wanted to include a story specifically about my mother in this book; however, I struggled to come up with events in which she was the central character. Then my wife, as usual, hit on the truth: my mother was always an important *supporting character*—like the Academy Awards category, she wins the Oscar for Best Supporting Role. A shy and modest introvert, it was the role she wanted. However, as you will learn from reading the stories, her influence was strong and her behind-the-scenes actions were irreplaceable, and there was never any doubt who really was in charge.

The response to my first book, *Wellfleet Tales,* has been gratifying and a bit overwhelming. Readers have thanked me for rekindling their memories, for telling them stories they never knew about their parents and grandparents, and for making them laugh (and in some cases, making them cry). The book and Facebook group, "Wellfleet Tales," have allowed old friends to reconnect and encouraged them to share even more stories with me; some of them are included in these pages.

Contributors to this book, directly and indirectly, are a long list, and I hope I don't exclude anyone. Thank you to Judy (Cochran) & Jack Delaney, Jon Lavash, Vern Costa, Ron Stewart, Suzanne (Grout) Thomas, Sharon (Murphy) Lottridge, Diane Silva-Salvador, Cynthia (Hood) Cocivera, Jim Hooker, Stewart

Armstrong, David Weintraub, Rick Alexander, Bill Holt, Janet Holt Cochrane, Gail (Russell) Bernard, Lee (Russell) Duff, Tom Russell, and all the little girls and boys (now "mature" adults) who attended Miss Judy's Wellfleet Dance Studio between 1953 and 1957.

    I thank the people who got me started writing about Wellfleet, encouraged my early attempts and kept me going: David Wright, the late Larry Peters, Don Thimas, and Jeff Tash, who published my first stories on his *Wellfleetian* blog. This book is dedicated to my family: my children, Jessica and Evan, who endured their father's story telling their whole lives, to my granddaughter, Eliana, who believes her "Bampy" can do no wrong; and mostly to my wife of forty-plus years (but who's counting), Ellen Keane, who may be sick of the stories, but loves Wellfleet almost as much as I do.

    The first story reflects some of her bewilderment at my ability to resurrect memories that would otherwise be long forgotten.

Wellfleet Memories – or – "Sorry I Asked"

"How do you remember all those people and stories—like all your elementary teachers?" asks my wife, "I couldn't tell you most of mine."

My wife is a city girl, growing up where anonymity was valued, and talking to strangers could end up with someone chasing you home. She is bewildered by the behavior of country folks; strangers waving to her as she drives past makes her nuts. Conversations about who was related to whom, and which was so-and-so's house, sound like Greek to her *citified* ears.

I attempted to answer her question: "Your teachers just showed up in school and taught; you never saw them again until the next school day. My teachers lived, shopped and went to church in Wellfleet. Sometimes their children were my playmates."

I got a skeptical look in return.

"For example, my kindergarten teacher was Mrs. Fleming, who married Police Chief Bill Fleming, and she was also the director of our church's Junior Choir. Her sister, Edith Atwood, was my first grade teacher; her daughter, Nancy Atwood, went to first grade with my sister, Nancy. Her husband, Henry, was on the school committee that first hired my father as principal in 1938, and he was a selectman when my mother was Town Accountant."

I continue, "My second grade teacher was Mrs. Morton, who was a widow, but then married Ed Dickey, who was a good friend of my father's and sang in the choir. She played the organ in our church and her sons, Bruce and Philip, were ahead of me in school. She was also the Youth Fellowship leader (we met at her house on Sunday nights); I got to watch Bonanza *in living color* 'cause she had one of the first color TVs in town."

Pausing for a breath . . . "Mrs. Peters taught third grade, while her husband, Joe, was the teaching Principal of the Truro Elementary School and a colleague of my father's. And then Mrs. Snow taught . . ."

"Okay . . . I get it . . . sorry I asked."

"And Mr. Bacon taught fifth grade, retired the next year . . . and then we had Mr. Ryder. He was fun, and a good teacher . . ." I look around, but my wife seems to have vanished. Well, she did ask.

Wellfleet in the Old Days

How We Got To There – Left – and Came Back

RICHARD A. COCHRAN
Mr. Cochran, Provincetown High School teacher, has been elected principal of the new Wellfleet Consolidated School succeeding R. Vernon Hays who resigned to accept another position.

Dick Cochran - Wellfleet Principal for twelve years 1938-1943 & 1952-1959

In the midst of the Great Depression my father brought our family to Cape Cod in 1937 when he accepted a job as a math teacher at Provincetown High School. Only one year later he became the teaching principal of the brand-new Wellfleet Consolidated School. Today we would be called "wash-ashores," a reference to something that rolled in with the tide. Back then my family (father, mother and sister Nancy) were just outsiders. Outsiders were subjects of suspicion, and the feeling that they didn't understand the way things were done on the Cape.

In 1939 my sister, Judy, was born at Cape Cod Hospital in Hyannis; however, that didn't make her a Cape native. To be a native of the Cape both you *and* your parents, two generations, need to be born on Cape Cod. Like the long-time Wellfleet native said at Town Meeting, *"I'm sick of these transients. They live here twenty or thirty years, change everything, then move away and stick us with the results!"* Guilty as charged, we were long-time transients, just some more wash-ashores!

Of course, being the principal of the only school in town gave my father a potentially respected position, but he had to earn it. Wellfleet had a history of driving principals out of the job in a year- or even less. When he was hired in 1938 from a field of 40 candidates, he became the sixth principal in five years. Wellfleet kids and their parents were tough! The fact that he stayed five years, leaving in 1943, was a testament to the degree to which he was accepted by citizens of the closed community. When he returned nine years later, in 1952, Wellfleet was relieved to get a proven principal who already knew the community, and they rewarded him with a salary of $4,200. But it certainly wasn't the salary that led him to teach at Wellfleet and Nauset until 1971; it was his genuine love of the Cape.

Why did Dick Cochran succeed and become popular, when other Wellfleet principals had fled the job as soon as possible? Basketball was a big factor. Cape Cod was a basketball hotbed, and sometimes the only sport a tiny high school could field. My father had been a basketball star at Medford High School, leading them to a state title, and then at Tufts College, where he had been Captain of some very good teams. He now took over as boys' basketball coach in Wellfleet and whipped them into a competitive squad.

Wellfleet was a hardscrabble fishing village, struggling to get by in a depression economy. Most residents were stubbornly proud and financially poor. Dick was the ninth of ten children (eight boys, two girls), and had only been ten years old in 1917, when his father, Charles Morton "Mort" Cochran, had died due to infection and complications from appendix surgery. His older siblings had worked to support the family and made it possible for the two youngest boys to go to Tufts on basketball scholarships. I believe the struggles of his childhood, the challenges of sports and having to scrap for everything, gave him the tools to fit in and thrive in Wellfleet.

This is a collection of stories that celebrate the good times and the fond memories; however, it's only fair to acknowledge that life is never all roses and lollipops. Every town has its conflicts, tragedies and scandals. The principal's family tried to stay out of the feuds, but it was often hard, and sometimes the principal was the center of the issue.

My mother felt that we needed to be extra well-behaved since any misbehavior would reflect on my father and his job. I know I felt the self-imposed pressure, and didn't feel free to let loose until I left Wellfleet and went to college. Having said all that, I believe Wellfleet was a special place, where the good offset and outweighed the inevitable negatives that are part of life.

A Perfect Day at the Beaches

I looked at my three oldest female cousins, Marsha, Gail and Lee, along with their boyfriends (and future husbands) Doug, George and Syd, "Okay, it's high tide down the bay 'bout 10:00 and low-tide at the back-shore round 4:00, so we got the perfect day. We'll head down to Mayo's for a swim, walk home for lunch, then head to Newcomb's in the afternoon to catch the waves, stop off at Gull Pond to wash off the salt, and be home in time for supper."

I was about twelve years old and well-practiced in my role as Wellfleet tour guide (a role my wife regrets that I have yet to relinquish to this day). My cousins and their boyfriends had made a day trip from Medford to go to the beach—but not just one beach, we were going to do the "grand tour." The bay is a delightful place to swim at high tide: a nice beach, calm waters, with scenic views of all types of boats. However, low tide exposed large expanses of mud-flats and sharp shells, and attracted the quahog diggers.

Just the opposite of the bay, the best time to swim at the ocean (we called it "the backshore") was low tide. The ocean at high tide is a tricky place; waves break right on the beach, there is a steep drop-off and potentially dangerous "undertow." Low tide at Newcomb Hollow, Lecount Hollow or Cahoon Hollow was ideal. The tide retreated from the steep tidal slope to the flat, sandy expanse of the low-tide level. Strong waves broke far out and traveled many yards before losing their power in the shallow water. It was safe for little children, yet exhilarating for teens and adults to body surf.

Cape Cod has the unique triple threat of ocean waves, sheltered bay beaches, and pristine fresh-water ponds. The Cape owes this to the glaciers that pushed the arm of the peninsula forward, creating an ocean side and a bay side. In addition, huge chunks of ice were marooned in the sandy residue as the glaciers melted and retreated. When the isolated, massive ice "bergs" eventually melted, they left deep depressions in the earth that collected water from ground streams and rainfall, and created what geologists term "kettle ponds."

A sixty foot whale washed ashore between Mayo Beach and Chequesset Country Club -circa 1966

Mayo Beach on the Bay

My mother on the left with Dorothy Connors, her good friend and our Hiller Ave neighbor, in front of Steve Daniels "Packet Port" cottages. Our house was behind the sand dune at the top of Taylor Hill.

Mayo Beach on Wellfleet Harbor extends for close to a mile, from the pier to the corner of Kendrick Ave. at the former site of Lorenzo Dow Baker's Chequesset Inn. It's the site of bay beaches, the Wellfleet Recreation Center and the landmark Bookstore Restaurant.

We swam at the far end, away from the pier, because it was a short walk down the hill from our house. The small beach was only used by the residents of the row of cottages. It was a great place to swim and a safe beach for little children.

That's me at the same beach, tall and skinny. I was not Charles Atlas.

The "Town Beach" is at the other end of Mayo's across from the ballfield and close to the pier. There was a time in the fifties when this beach was more active than it is now. John Rogers remembers a raft for swimmers anchored off the shore, and Sharon Murphy recalls the snack stand (hot dogs for a quarter) and Al Graham's bar and restaurant. For several years in the fifties it was the location of the swimming lesson program run by the town recreation commission.

Around 1956-57 several Wellfleet teens organized an informal water ski club. David Whiting had a boat and all the ski equipment, and encouraged some of his high-school friends, including Judy, to take up the sport. David was very accomplished and could perform advanced tricks and stunts, including skiing on a round disk while standing on his head.

They usually skied off the town beach near the pier, although they also skied on Gull Pond which in those years allowed motor boats. Judy remembers an exciting event that, in the end, left her less than thrilled: the Boston NBC news affiliate decided to do a feature story on the new craze of water skiing and contacted the Orleans ski club to do some filming. Word had spread of David Whiting's tricks, so the Wellfleet club was invited to join the group.

The camera crew filmed the more experienced skiers and got some great shots of David doing a headstand. Then the news people decided they wanted to get film of a group of girls skiing in tandem. At this point Judy had only skied three or four times, but she got in the middle of four girls from Orleans.

The girls had to takeoff from the dock, a new experience for Judy, and she and several others failed in the first attempt. On the second try all the girls got up and the five took off through the choppy bay waters with the camera crew filming it all.

Judy on the Ski Club float - July 4th

When Judy got home, she breathlessly told her mother, father and grandmother that they had to watch the evening news to see her water skiing. The family gathered around the black-and-white TV and waited for the big event. On came the reporter with the story about the water skiing craze. Camera footage featured David doing his amazing tricks, and then, for the finale, the five girls appeared. The Orleans girls waved to the camera, skied out to the sides and jumped the wake in an impressive display of control. Meanwhile, the girl in the middle, Judy, was bent over the rope, hanging on for dear life, and looking like the water-ski version of a rodeo clown.

Judy's cheesecake – Town Beach

The Ponds

"The happy family" at Long Pond circa 1941, Judy's crying, my mother is ready to wring her neck, and Nancy and my father are not smiling. In the background is the "ice ramp" that used pulleys to raise up huge blocks of ice for summer refrigeration.

Gull Pond, Long Pond and Great Pond are the largest fresh water bodies in Wellfleet. Each has its unique charm and features, each has its own fans and supporters. In the early days it seems that Long Pond was the most popular. I suspect this was because a road went right past its sandy beach "public landing". Great Pond has a steep embankment and Gull Pond is down a side road that in the old days was probably just a cart path, so Long Pond was the most easily accessible. The only pond in old family photos (from before I was born) is Long Pond.

When we moved back to Wellfleet, I remember that Long Pond seemed our preferred location when I was little. It's ideal for a family with children. Parents can sit at the edge of the water and the incline is gradual, giving toddlers plenty of room

Long Pond 2010 - The stairs seem to be in the same location as the old "ice ramp." - photo Rick Cochran

to splash without getting over their heads. The small raft gave the older kids a place to play and sunbathe, while it gave improving swimmers a destination goal to test their prowess. I believe Long Pond was the location for the first recreational program's swimming lessons. However, swimming lessons for little ones required an area to be roped off, and the smaller beach of Long Pond didn't provide much room for lessons and swimmers to share. For a time in the early fifties, swimming lessons were moved to the bay at the end of Mayo Beach.

Long Pond 2010 - The raft presented a destination challenge for novice swimmers - photo Rick Cochran

When a good road was paved to Gull Pond, its larger parking area and wider beach area led to it replacing Long Pond as the most popular fresh-water location in town. Around the mid-fifties, Wellfleet moved its swimming lessons to Gull Pond. This was a smart move: at the bay, lessons had had to be scheduled based on the tides, and on a windy day the choppy water could be intimidating for the six year olds just learning to stick their faces in the water to blow bubbles.

Some of my fondest memories are of swimming at Gull Pond. It could get crowded, but for a little kid this also meant having lots of playmates. Gull had a large raft that was mounted on pier pilings. The raft was perfect for games of tag, jumping into the water, climbing out, and jumping in again to avoid becoming "it." The close side of the raft was shallow enough for young children and non-swimmers, while the far side was deep enough for diving and more advanced swimmers.

Free swimming lessons by a Red Cross-certified instructor was a strong attraction for parents. My sister Judy taught swimming the summer of 1960, after her junior year in college. To get certified she had to undertake an intensive period of training and testing. Lessons ran for a two-week period and covered ability levels from beginner to lifesaving.

At the beginning of one new session, a summer visitor signed up her two young boys. The minimum age limit was six years old, and the first boy looked about right. Judy asked his age and the mother said, "Six." The tiny brother came next, and skeptically, Judy asked his age, "Six!" said the mother adamantly. Well, there was no requirement to show birth certificates, so Judy just went along with it.

The first day the lesson went fine, but the next day, Judy led the beginners in blowing bubbles. The bigger brother blew bubbles easily, but the littler brother refused. When Judy tried to encourage him, he put his hands on his hips, gave a defiant look, and said, "How do you expect me to do that? After all, I'm only four!"

Judy glanced over at the shocked look on the mother's face, as the little boy ran to her arms. The mother and boys never returned for swimming lessons.

Gull Pond and the raft - Rick Cochran 2010

One memory was burned indelibly in my young brain. The Gull Pond raft was originally anchored on pilings that kept it above the water level of spring and early summer. As the summer wore on, the water level dropped, creating a gap of several inches between the bottom support beams and the top of the water and a bigger gap under the floorboards. This created a breathable hiding place under the raft, and it was great for kids to play; we ducked under the raft and came up in the open area. From there, we were free to walk around under the length of the raft without being seen from above. "Tag" could be played on the raft, in the water, and under the raft.

When I was around eleven, I was hanging out under the raft, hiding from the world, and spying through the open space between the water and the support beams. At the north end of the beach two young couples arrived, most likely young men from the North Truro Air Force Radar base and their dates. The women were dressed in daring swim suits for the era, something between two-piece and bikinis, and they filled them out with voluptuous curves.

The men jumped in the water, splashing and cavorting, and made their way to the side of the raft where I was keeping my unobserved watch. Both guys boosted themselves onto the raft, and called out for the girlfriends to join them. The first young woman waded to the side of the raft directly in front of my inquisitive eyes. She decided she couldn't boost herself onto the raft, and so she reached her arms high for her boyfriend to pull her up, which he did with a vigorous tug. Well . . . her arms reached up . . . her body rose up . . . her bathing suit top rose up . . . *but* two other objects did not, in fact they followed the rules of gravity, where they ended up staring back into the wide eyes of the 11-year-old boy only inches away.

Some educational experiences you can't get in school.

The Back-Shore

Growing up in Wellfleet I'm an admitted beach snob. I'm also a hopeless bore when it comes to the correct language usage regarding shellfish and water bodies. A quahog is not a steamer, and neither one is merely a "clam." A scallop is a sc-<u>all</u>-op and not a sc-<u>al</u>-op; double letter L makes it "all," not "al." Wellfleet Harbor is not the ocean, it's the bay, as is Nantucket *Sound* and Cape Cod *Bay*. The only ocean is the Atlantic, which thunders against the eastern side of the lower Cape. However, in Wellfleet we didn't call it the ocean, it was the *back-shore*.

In the fifties there were three major back-shore beaches: Cahoon Hollow, LeCount Hollow (also known as Maguire's Landing), and Newcomb Hollow. Hollows are just what they sound like, lower depressions in the midst of the continuous flow of sand dunes, which allow easier access to the beach. All three are great beaches with varying advantages and disadvantages that change over the years. When I was young, Newcomb was the preferred beach, maybe because it had a larger parking lot that took a bit longer to fill up. As a teenager it was the place to go because it was where most of the other teenagers went.

In that era we enjoyed the beach, dunes and clay cliffs, mindless of the environmental mayhem we were creating. We climbed the dunes and ran or rolled down, got up and did it again.

We pulled clumps of red clay out of the scattered outcrops, broke it into pieces and threw them at each other in impromptu battles. We walked the paths at the tops of the dunes through the bear berries and clusters of brush and pitch pine, occasionally surprising a sun bather who was seeking privacy for a full body tan. In summary, we had a blast!

As teenagers we headed to our self-selected, designated area, fifty yards to the right, where all the teenagers gathered. Boys and girls came and went depending on their summer work schedules. Footballs were tossed and waves were body surfed, but mostly we hung out, some as couples, but mostly with the boys ogling the girls and the girls preening and doing a good job of looking pretty and getting attention.

LeCount Hollow had a small parking lot and a large collection of nearby homes and cottages. Laurie Cardinal was a year ahead of me in school, and her parents owned a house and cottage colony on the dune to south of the entrance. On a recent visit to the beach in 2014, I was amazed at the evidence of how far the dunes have eroded. I knew they had, but now the Cardinal's former home is creeping dangerously close to the edge.

Cahoon Hollow was the home of the old Coast Guard Station which was turned into a snack shack and eventually the restaurant, bar, and busy night club that it is now. The summer of 1969 I was working as night watchman on the town pier, and in August my friend, Tom Murphy, turned 21, an auspicious occasion marked by the fact that he could now legally drink. Obviously, a trip to the Beachcomber was required to celebrate the occasion. Only one problem: my birthday wasn't until September, and I was still twenty. Tom and his older brothers, Mac and Bruce, assured me there was no problem. In those days your driver's license was just a piece of cardboard without a photo. So we went to the club, and everyone else showed their IDs at the door and went inside. I snuck around to the side window where Tom handed me his driver's license, then I went to the door, showed the ID and got into the bar.

The Beachcomb restaurant and night club uses the old Coast Guard building - postcard

The View – The Target Ship – The Great Blackout

Our view in the fifties – Mayo Beach – town pier top left – Indian Neck top right.

Our house had an amazing panoramic view of Wellfleet Harbor and out into Cape Cod Bay. To the right was all of Great Island and Jeremy's Point, to the left was the town pier, Indian Neck, the breakwater and the shore of Eastham. On a clear day, at low tide, you could make out the outline of a peculiar vessel, the *target ship*.

S.S. Longstreet known as the "Target Ship"

This ship was originally the S.S. Longstreet, a merchant marine craft that was severely damaged by storms, and ultimately designated for use in aerial target practice. It was purposely towed to a shallow area off the Eastham/Wellfleet line and run aground after WWII.

The target ship often provided evening entertainment that rivaled the greatest fireworks displays. Periodically the Air Force and Naval Aviation ran night-time practice bombing runs with spectacular booms and flashes of light. In the early sixties the frequency of the practice seemed to increase for an extended period of time. A few years later my father told me that there had been a connection to the Cuban Missile Crisis of 1962 during the Kennedy Administration, a period of time in October when the world teetered on the edge of nuclear warfare.

The Soviets had denied they had sent missiles to Cuba, but were embarrassed when our United Nations Ambassador, Adlai Stevenson, revealed detailed photos that clearly showed launching pads and missiles under construction. Evidently we used flash aerial photography to get the pictures, a technique that had been developed and refined by practicing on the target ship.

Our view from Taylor Hill gave us a unique perspective on another scary event. On the early evening of November 9, 1965 we lost our electricity. This was a common event in windswept Wellfleet; however, it was a beautiful, calm evening without wind or storms. My father looked out our picture window and saw a chilling sight. Normally our evening view showed lights along the entire north coast of Cape Cod, almost all the way to the canal. Instead of flickering lights he saw nothing—no light anywhere—other than that of a rising full moon. It was the *Great Northeast Blackout of 1965* that left parts of Ontario, New Jersey, New York, Connecticut, Rhode Island, New Hampshire, Vermont, Massachusetts and over 30 million people without power for up to 13 hours.

My wife was then a teenager in urban Arlington, Massachusetts, and she remembers it as inconvenient, but not particularly upsetting, because without TV or radio they had no idea the extent of the blackout and thought it was just limited to their part of town. Just the opposite for us; we could see for scores of miles, and my father had admitted after the power was restored that he was convinced nuclear war had broken out, and the Soviets had exploded a missile that wiped out the electrical power. Fortunately he was wrong.

Names & Nicknames

With a population of just over one thousand, a few multi-generational families dominated the last names. There were so many Taylors at the corner of Cove Road and Rte. 6 that it was referred to as the "Taylor Jungle." Other common names were: Rose, Berrio, Wiles, Valli, Paine, Frazier, Hopkins, Snow, Pierce, Newcomb, Baker, Gross, Rich and Atwood.

In Wellfleet a lot of men, and some women, went by their nicknames. Often I had no idea what their real names were. Here are just a few from the fifties and sixties:

Buddy Berrio Sr.	Buster (Ansel) Valli
Buddy (Edwin) Berrio Jr.	Pick (Alfred) Pickard
Bogsy Berrio	Soupy (David) Whiting
Chickie (Charles) Berrio	Wee Dalby
Tink (Robert) Taylor	Bud (Lenny) Gates
Honk Taylor	Skip (Howard) Dickey
Hap Taylor	Flip (Philip) Morton
Tito Moran	Putt Menangas
Houdini (Earl) Harding	Bunny Ellis
Duffy (Lawrence) Gardinier	Pinky Newcomb
Froggy Frazier	Rainey Kimec
Bubba Frazier	Gump Anderson
Blocky (Joe) Burgess	Barney (Everett) Adams
Pokey (Howard) Snow	Butch Davis
Rusty Rowell	Bunkie (Sharon) Murphy
Veeni (Slyvanus) Pierce	Babe (Cynthia) Hood
Bing (Warren) Harrington	Muffet (Stephanie) Blakely

Sometimes It Hurts To Be A Paine!

The old-time names are reflected throughout Wellfleet's geography: Taylor Hill, Mayo Beach, Gross Hill Rd., Dyers Pond, Newcomb Hollow, Cahoon Hollow, Paine Hollow and many more.

When my parents had just moved to Wellfleet in 1938, they went out for a Sunday drive, and literally ran into a car driven by Ben Paine that was overloaded with all his family. Ben drove the Wellfleet school bus and owned an auto repair shop on Briar Lane, so my father knew him well. Dad filled out the insurance form that asked repetitive and mundane questions.

-Where was the accident?   Paine Hollow, Wellfleet
- What was the street?   Paine Hollow Road
- Who was the other driver?   Ben Paine
- Who were the other passengers? Ken Paine, Betty Paine, -- Paine, -- Paine, -- Paine
- Do you have any other comments?
>My father couldn't resist. "This accident has been a real Paine," he wrote.

****

Judy Eicher was working at the Book Store when she noticed Bob and Sarah Paine crossing the street toward the restaurant. She commented, "Oh, here come the Paines." A new waitress looked at her and asked, "Are they really that bad?"

Wellfleet Politics

Wellfleet was not always the liberal, artistic community that we see today; back in the fifties, it was just the opposite. In 1952 Wellfleet and almost all of Cape Cod was a conservative Republican stronghold. Provincetown was the only lower-Cape community that had any serious Democrat representation. The Cape's voting reflected the general trend of rural areas supporting the GOP, with more urban areas backing the Democrats.

In the 1952 election 599 Wellfleet voters favored the Republican presidential winner, Dwight "Ike" Eisenhower and Vice President, Richard Nixon, while 111 voted for the Democrat, Adlai Stevenson and his running mate, John Sparkman of Alabama. The Republican candidate for governor, Christian Herter, ousted the Democratic Governor, Paul Dever, with the help of Wellfleet, who voted 564-142 for the GOP challenger. In a race with future implications, Democrat John F. Kennedy upset the incumbent Republican Senator of Massachusetts, Henry Cabot Lodge Jr., despite Wellfleet's overwhelming support for the losing candidate: 527 Lodge to 178 Kennedy. Kennedy did a little better in Wellfleet than other Democrats that year, perhaps because his family owned the "Kennedy Compound" in Hyannis.

Charlie Bean

In my first book, *Wellfleet Tales*, I devoted a longer chapter to the legendary Charlie Bean. Charlie was a mentally challenged individual who would have been institutionalized if he hadn't been taken in as a child by a Wellfleet relative. Instead he was raised in town and "adopted" by the village. Charlie was an iconic character. Town folks swapped stories of Charlie's activities on a regular basis. Although he was illiterate and uneducated, my father said, "Charlie was as dumb as a fox." You couldn't put much over on him, and somehow he usually gained the upper hand.

Suzanne Grout Thomas relates some yarns about Charlie that weren't in my first book. In the old days Charlie delivered all the telegrams in town. He couldn't read, but he knew where everyone lived. Suzanne's Uncle, Win Downs, took advantage of this to orchestrate a practical joke. In the winter of 1942, Beulah Downs (Suzanne's mother and Win's sister) brought her roommate, Jean Torrey, home to Wellfleet from Bridgewater State Teachers College to celebrate Jean's birthday. Win was home from prep school, but sent a birthday message to Jean, knowing that Charlie Bean would be the *bearer* of the telegram. After dinner the doorbell rang, and Win urged Jean to answer it. She opened the door to the sight of a diminutive, grinning, jugged-eared Charlie Bean, bearing the telegram which he proudly handed to her. She opened the dispatch which read, *Happy Birthday Jean, Love, from the Bearer."*

In 1946 Suzanne's recently married parents moved back to Beulah's home town of Wellfleet. Beulah's father, Cyril Downs, purchased an old barn on West Main Street next to the curtain factory, which is now the library. The barn was turned into an apartment residence, with Suzanne's father, Channing Grout, providing the "sweat equity" by doing finish work in the house. Every day there was a knock on the door, and there was Charlie Bean. He'd walk in without a word, go into each of the four rooms, and jump up and down on the floors as hard as he could. As he left, Charlie turned to Channing and spoke his only words, "It'll do ya . . . b-y-y-y God."

On August 3, 1967, Charlie Bean died at the age of 74. I can think of no more fitting farewell words to Charlie than to repeat his signature phrase he said to almost anyone who spoke to him. No matter what they said, he would reply, filling in the appropriate name: *"By God you're right (Charlie)!"*

Tony's Barbershop

Location of Tony's, later Prudential R.E.

Sometimes it's not easy being *the* principal in a small town. Everybody knows every little thing that's going on, and everybody has an expert opinion on the topic. Tony's barbershop, like most barbershops, was a center for news and gossip, but with an additional feature. In the back of Tony's was a pool hall, strictly a males-only room that in the fifties was considered slightly disreputable, at least not the kind of place where the school principal would feel welcome. I suspect my father "bit his tongue" while getting his haircut from Tony, listening to the barber's expert opinion on all topics including education, all the time watching the young men, some still his students, going in and out of the pool hall with lit cigarettes dangling from their lips.

I got my first haircut from Tony, an event that I dreaded, but survived. Tony wasn't exactly "warm and cuddly"; he had a sharp tongue, and wasn't very patient. However, I think he was making some effort to be less harsh with a first-timer. What I really loved about the barbershop was the greatest collection of comic books I'd ever seen. When my turn came to get my hair cut I was always disappointed to put down Superman, Batman, or Archie and Jughead.

It started with an issue over basketball, the only sport at Wellfleet High School in the fifties and the center of interest for the whole community. In the 1953-54 season the Wellfleet boys had a terrific team with three Cape League All-Stars: Gene Howland, Ted Bedell and "Tink" Taylor. However, in 1954-55 too many boys had been academically ineligible and there weren't enough players to field a team. Certain members of the community felt the principal should have "manipulated" grades so Wellfleet didn't have to forfeit the whole season; certainly, some of the ineligible players probably felt that way.

For a couple of years we got our hair cut by Tony and all was well, but one day that changed. Some former "students" came out of the backroom and gave my father dirty looks, while mumbling under their breath. Tony couldn't resist, and started to offer his views on what should've been done—and that was it! My father was generally easygoing, but you could only push him so far and then he snapped. Well, Tony got an earful, and unpleasant words were exchanged. Then I was extracted from my comic books and we were out the door.

Soon after, my mother purchased a pair of clippers, and we never went to the barbershop again. Unfortunately, my mother's initial skills were limited to running the clippers over my head, producing a result somewhat like that of army recruit boot camp. It brought me to tears the first time I viewed my shaved head in the mirror. Eventually she improved and was able to give me an acceptable version of the "whiffle" cut that was then in style.

    One day I was in Wellfleet Center, and spotted Tony sitting on the steps of his shop waiting for a customer. Being a naïve little boy, I walked by, smiled and waved, but Tony turned his back and went inside. I was left a bit puzzled, but what I really missed was the comic books.

Crime and Punishment
The Wellfleet PD

Thief Snatches Tree At South Wellfleet

SOUTH WELLFLEET, April 16—A thief of the meaner sort still was unidentified today after uprooting and carrying off a young spruce tree from the lawn of Mr. and Mrs. Charles E. Paine of South Wellfleet.

The theft, which occurred early Monday night, was committed by a man wearing a long, light-colored coat. Mrs. Paine rapped on her window when she saw the shrub thief making off with his loot, but he jumped into a truck he had parked nearby and drove off.

Ron Stewart found this article from the 1930s. Fortunately, the thief didn't have a white beard, wasn't wearing a red suit or driving a reindeer sleigh.

In Volume Four of Ruth Rickmers' wonderful series, *Wellfleet Remembered,* she details the history of the Wellfleet police force. Prior to 1938, "constables and occasional summer patrolmen were the law enforcement officials of the town." At that year's Town Meeting voters established the first police department, with the chairman of the board of selectman designated as the Chief of Police with no additional compensation. The first non-uniformed, non-professional and unpaid chiefs were John Daniels, Charlie Frazier and Lawrence "Duffy" Gardinier.

In 1938 the first two police officers were Ruth Wiles Rickmer's father, Elmer Wiles, and George E. Berrio. The first professional Police Chief was a retired

Chief Bill Felming with Wellfleet's first cruiser, a 1949 Pontiac - photo from "Wellfleet Remembered Vol 4" by Ruth (Wiles) Rickmers

Massachusetts State Police Trooper, William Fleming, who served from 1946 to 1954. (Chief Fleming was married to my kindergarten teacher, Hilda (Baker) Fleming.)

Frank Davenport, an experienced police officer from Brockton, took over in 1954 and served almost twelve years until 1965. I remember Chief Davenport as a quiet, tall and imposing figure, who bore a striking resemblance to John Wayne. Some remember he had a limp, the result of a stabbing injury he suffered on the Brockton PD. Howie Dykeman took over briefly in 1965 before Charlie Silva became chief from 1965-1969.

In the 1967 Town Report, Chief Silva notes the "great numbers of hippies, surfers and campers . . . sleeping and camping on private land and beaches . . . many with no money . . . and the increased number of thefts from cars." [Author's note: In those days most of those cars were probably unlocked . . . not that it was an excuse!]

1951 PD Left-Right-Albert Rose, Charles Silva, Elmer Wiles, Seraphine Rego, Anthony Oliver, Chief Fleming - photo "Wellfleet Remembered Vol 4" Ruth (Wiles) Rickmers

Front-Dick Huntley, Chief Charlie Silva, Paul Lussier- Rear- Austin Turnbull, John Weinig, Bobby Adams – photo Diane Silva Salvador circa 1966

Chief Davenport and Officer Bob White with the new 1959 cruiser - photo "Wellfleet Remembered Vol 4" Ruth (Wiles) Rickmers

Law & Order at the Pier or Don't *** With Charlie

In my first *Wellfleet Tales* book I included two stories about my summer in 1969 as the Assistant Harbormaster/Night Watchman at the Wellfleet Marina. My Nauset classmate, Rick Alexander, had worked there before me in the summers of 1966 & '67. Rick worked for his father, Harbormaster Charlie Alexander, and did more day shifts than I did, resulting in several great stories.

One of the timeless pastimes at the Wellfleet Marina is watching the would-be boaters launching, or attempting to launch, by backing down the ramp next to the Harbormaster's shack. Suzanne Grout Thomas remembers her family picking up dinner at one of the pier's food places and watching this free and often hilarious entertainment.

Harbor Master's shack with the boat ramp right front - Rick Cochran 2010

Rick Alexander remembers one novice boat owner in particular. A summer visitor, this young New York City school teacher arrived at the launch ramp on a busy Saturday. Flushed with pride over his brand new 16-foot outboard, he paid his fee. Then Rick watched as the boating newcomer repeatedly, and haplessly, tried to back his boat trailer down the ramp. With a long line forming, and other boat owners getting frustrated, Rick finally offered to back it down for him. The owner happily accepted and after Rick had backed it down, our "sailor" finished unloading his shiny new boat. Then he drove his car and empty trailer up the ramp and went to park, leaving his young wife holding the bow rope.

Rick went off to help somewhere else, only to hear screams: "My boat! . . . My boat!" Rushing back to the ramp Rick saw the boat drifting away from the pier, with the wife still holding the end of the rope,

Wellfleet Marina - Rick Cochran 2010

which not been secured to the boat. Now that would have been bad enough, but as the boat headed out into the harbor, the hull sank noticeably lower into the water. Rick turned to the New Yorker, "Did you put the drain plugs in?" he asked. "What drain plugs," was the response.

By the time Rick got his own boat from the other side of the pier and went out to retrieve the ill-fated motor launch, it was almost submerged. Our poor boat owner had to spend a great deal of money to salvage his sunken, but still never-used boat from the harbor.

Another time two guys cut in front of four or five other boats in line. The other boaters put up a protest, and Charlie told Rick to pull them out of line because "their boat needed to be inspected." The harbormaster then proceed to conduct the most thorough inspection of any boat known to man: life jackets, anchor, ropes, even seats. He thought he saw a defective bolt on the outboard, so he made them take the motor off, and then Charlie did a microscopic analysis of the engine's working parts. The whole process took about two hours. The good news was that by the time the men launched their boat, the line was gone.

Charlie Alexander took his harbormaster duties seriously, and on the pier his word was law. Another day a man backed his trailer down the ramp, then told Charlie he'd pay after he parked. The harbormaster told Rick he had "a funny feeling," and asked his son to go down to the boat and pull out the keys. Sure enough, the man came back and quickly jumped in his boat, then pushed off and gave Charlie and Rick a wave that involved raising his hand and extending his middle finger. Then he yelled, "Where are my keys?" Charlie held them up, "You mean these . . . I guess you should've paid the ramp fee." He threw the keys out into the water as far as possible. Although they had a "float" attached, it took the man forever to find them.

Even gangsters had to bow to Charlie's law. In 1966 a luxury yacht pulled into the marina and tied up in the spot of Captain Jack's tourist fishing boat, the *Naviator*. Rick went down and explained that they couldn't dock there, because it was the permanent home of Captain Jack, who would soon be back with his load of tourists. The owner, a fancy dresser with a beautiful blonde on each arm, gave Rick a look, "Tough ***, I'll dock wherever I want!" A limousine pulled up and the big-shot and two blondes got in the back while the driver held the door. After closing the door, the driver informed Rick that the man was connected to the mob.

Rick called his dad, who said, "I'll be right down." When the harbormaster arrived he sized up the situation, untied the bow and stern lines, gave the boat a shove and watched it drift into the harbor. "Call me when they get back," he told his son. When Rick reminded him who the guy was, Charlie said, "I don't care if he's President of the United States; rules are rules!"

Meanwhile, the boat drifted away and got hung up on the jetty. When the limo returned the owner went ballistic, demanding to know who had untied his yacht. Rick claimed ignorance and told him by the time he'd seen it the boat was too far away to get. Then he gave the limo driver directions to the breakwater and told them they better hurry before it got stranded, and off went the limo, burning rubber in its haste.

Rick admits he ignored his father's orders to call him when the owner returned. His better judgment told him he didn't want his dad at the bottom of the harbor wearing cement boots. However, the harbormaster got the final word, which went something like, "Don't *** with Charlie!"

The Halloween Prank

Sharon ("Bunkie" Murphy) Lottridge offers this memory of Halloween and the way things were handled in the old days.

On Halloween of 1960, Sharon and a co-conspirator were too old for "trick or treat," but not too old for "tricks." Together with their *partners in crime*, two young men from the North Truro Air Force radar installation, they planned the ultimate in Halloween pranks. The young people piled into a big, white Bonneville Pontiac, and drove from Truro to Provincetown collecting signs from the (closed for the season) motels along the way, and stuffed them into the trunk of the big car.

The target of the prank was long-time Wellfleet Police Chief Frank Davenport, who lived on a quiet and isolated back road. The conspirators were confident that Chief Davenport would be occupied patrolling the main areas of town during the hectic Halloween night. The idea was to leave the motel signs in Chief Davenport's front yard, and make a hasty get-away: a brilliant and brazen plan.

The foursome decided that it might look suspicious if the white Bonneville was parked too long in front of the house. So, with a flip of a coin, near-sighted Bunkie was selected to place the signs. With craft and stealth, the car pulled up to the Chief's house, and with her heart pounding, our heroine jumped out and quickly unloaded the signs, then watched the Pontiac pull away, with the driver planning to make a leisurely loop and return to pick up our culprit.

Bunkie planted the signs in the Chief's front yard with speed and efficiency, then hid behind a tree across the street. Almost immediately the big white car cruised up the deserted road and slowed in front of the house. Anxious to make her escape, Bunkie jumped out from behind the tree and waved her arms frantically for her friends to stop. She ran to the car, opened the door, hopped in the front seat, and came face-to-face with . . . Chief Davenport, who was driving his own big white car back to his house.

The next day the four conspirators exchanged a flurry of panicked phone calls. Our heroine agreed to take the fall (the Air Force men would have faced serious punishment from the base commander), and Sharon was the only one who had been caught. That afternoon, a Wellfleet police cruiser showed up at her house. She started to get in the front seat, but was told, "prisoners sit in the back!" At the Chief's house, Sharon collected the signs from his yard and the cruiser headed to Truro, where she returned them to the motels. To her further humiliation, a Provincetown police cruiser met them at the town line, where custody of Sharon and the signs was transferred so she could complete her task throughout Ptown. Finally finished, she was transferred to a Truro cruiser and delivered to her father, who was working at a building in that town. We'll skip over the not-so-happy family reunion!

Fifty-six years have passed; the Statute of Limitations has expired. After intense interrogation by this author, Sharon still refuses to name the Air Force men. However, under terrifying threats she has finally divulged one name: Betty Paine, you can come out of hiding now.

Wellfleet's Outlaws - Kid Costa and Bonnie & Clyde

Vern Costa -FBI most wanted poster circa 1948 - just kidding!

In the late 1940s, five-year-old Vern Costa pulled off a bold caper. Vern got a complete cowboy outfit for his birthday: chaps, vest, cowboy hat, double holster and cap pistols. Inspired by movie westerns, he concocted a daring plan. In full regalia, "The Kid" walked down the street to the Wellfleet Savings Bank, pulled a bandana up to cover his face, and walked in with cap pistols blazing. "Stick'em up!" declared the mini-bandit. The pint-sized desperado didn't get the money, just laughs from the tellers. Years later, Vern became a teacher and coach in Bourne. (Obviously, he was hired before criminal background checks were required.)

Scene of the Crime - Wellfleet Savings Bank - Our Lady of Lourdes to the left

Diana Silva and David Francis were the *Bonnie and Clyde* of the elementary-age set. Diane, daughter of future Wellfleet Police Chief Charlie Silva, admits that she and David stole fluorescent colored sun glasses from the Wellfleet News store. Wracked with guilt, the two headed to *Our Lady of Lourdes* Catholic Church to confess their sin to Father Dennis. To their surprise and chagrin, the priest stepped out of the confessional, grabbed the two by their ears and marched them back to Wellfleet News to return the glasses and apologize to Rusty and Cliff.

The Wellfleet News store in 2010, scene of the great sunglasses theft.

I am confessing, for the first time, my own *breaking and entering* offense, committed when I was about twelve. At the junction of Chequesset Neck Road and Hamblin Farm Road is a stately old home that was once owned by someone connected with Lorenzo Dow Baker, *The Banana King* and owner of the Chequesset Inn.

Jay Sherwin told me that some of the boys found an open basement window and explored the fascinating house. On a dare, I slipped inside with several friends and found an unofficial museum. The Bakers had been big supporters of Teddy Roosevelt when he had run for another term as President, on the *Bull Moose Party* ticket. In the stairwell was a giant portrait of Teddy delivering a vigorous speech, and the bedrooms were filled with Roosevelt campaign pins and other memorabilia. It was my only trip inside and soon afterward I heard that some of the boys had been caught. To their credit, I guess they kept the code of silence and never ratted me out.

Family – Summer Friends – Wellfleet Activities
Nana

"Mamie, you get down off that ladder," said my mother to my 84-year-old grandmother. Nana was half-way up the rickety, wooden step ladder with a bottle of Windex and a roll of paper towels. For several weeks she had asked my father to wash the salty sea spray off our huge picture-window, so she could admire the magnificent view, and watch the sailboat races on Wellfleet Harbor. My father often operated on the motto, "Don't put off for tomorrow what you can put off until next week," and he had "yessed" his mother-in-law to death until the feisty octogenarian couldn't wait any longer.

My mother used Nana's first name whenever she delivered a serious message; however, she knew that *ordering* her stubborn mother to do something was a waste of breath. Now she thought of a different strategy, "Do you know how much it would cost to replace that picture window if you slip and crack it? It would be hundreds of dollars!"

My grandmother paused and deliberated, "Well, I wouldn't want to cost you any money, but I do wish Dick would wash this window. Can't see a thing since that last storm."

With that, Nana climbed down the ladder, handed the Windex and towels to my mother and went back inside the house. That evening, my father washed the window.

Throughout my life, Nana was a constant presence, helping to care for me from the time I was born. When we moved back to Wellfleet in 1952, she left her apartment in Medford for the summers to watch me, so my mother could work seasonal jobs to supplement the modest family income. Around 1960, when I was twelve, Nana came to live with us year-round, and my mother took a full-time job at the Wellfleet Post Office.

Elizabeth Mae (Taylor) Riley was born in Bloomfield, Connecticut in 1882, eight years younger than her next oldest sibling, and a surprise to her 48-year-old father and 36-year-old mother. A self-described "spoiled brat," she was doted on by her much older siblings, and was a special favorite of her father, Union Civil War veteran, Charles Lambert Taylor.

Nana had never liked the name Elizabeth, because the nickname, "Lizzie" was too evocative of the infamous Lizzie Borden. So, throughout her life she had used her middle name, Mae, or her nickname, Mamie. We teased that if she'd used her real name, she would have been Elizabeth Taylor, like the glamorous movie star. I'm not sure Nana thought that would've been a good thing. A staunch Republican, she much preferred that her nickname was the same as the First Lady of the country, Mamie Eisenhower.

I've been reminded many times that I was a special "pet," and could do no wrong in my grandmother's eyes. When I was sixteen, a new driver with only a few weeks of experience, I managed to crash the family car into a telephone pole near the Eastham Town Hall. Fortunately, I was only going about ten mph as we exited the parking lot after one of the Eastham teen dances. Gene Casey, Brian Ramsdell and I survived, but the station wagon needed a new radiator. When Nana explained the accident to people, somehow the telephone pole had leaped out into my path, and clearly it had not been my fault.

Nana was a life-long Methodist, and it was an adjustment for her to adapt to the Congregational Church my family attended. The church had two ladies clubs, the Needle Craft for women my mother's age, and the Ladies Aid Society for the older ladies. She settled in comfortably with the older group. One of those Wellfleet ladies, probably the only one with a driver's license, picked up several of the women and drove them to the club meetings. My mother was very uncomfortable with this arrangement, but with her work schedule she couldn't drive Nana herself. Besides, Nana, who had never driven and didn't have a license, assured my mother that the woman "drove just fine!"

I didn't understand my mother's concern until one day I observed, first-hand, the driving of Nana's friend. I was walking home from the town center on Chequesset Neck Road when I saw a familiar car coming toward me. The passenger-side wheels of the car were on the sandy shoulder of the road, as the elderly driver crept along at 20 mph. Fortunately, I was on the other side of the street, or I would have had to make a run-for-it. To my amazement the car continued, creeping closer and closer to a telephone pole that was dead-ahead. Just before an imminent collision, the driver swerved out on to the road, cleared the pole, but then turned the wheel and went back onto the shoulder once again. She continued on this course until she approached the next telephone pole, swerved out onto the road, then back onto the shoulder. I stood in shock as the car, with my grandmother in it, continued down Chequessett Neck, ducking in and out between the poles.

When Nana moved in with us she knew nothing about baseball. I was already a long-suffering Red Sox fan and watched most of the games on TV. When Nana learned that Red Sox star pitcher Bill Monbouquette was from her native town of Medford, Massachusetts, she became interested. She couldn't pronounce his name; it came out something like Mum-bo-gret, so she, like most fans, just called him Mombo. Soon, I was teaching her the intricacies of double plays and sacrifice flies, and the rules of the game. In no time at all she was an opinionated fan. When local boy Tony Conigliaro, from Lynn, arrived on the team as a teenager, Nana was enamored. Once again she couldn't pronounce his name, but in her eyes Tony C. could do no wrong.

One player she never liked was *my* favorite player, Carl Yastrzemski. Another Red Sox star with an unpronounceable name, Nana only focused on his negatives. While he was winning batting titles and making spectacular plays in left field, she only saw the times he made outs or hit into double plays. In 1967, Yaz was single-handedly leading the Red Sox on their "Impossible Dream," from ninth place to the American League pennant. I was home for part of the summer after my freshman year of college, and watching a late-August game with Nana.

With men on base and two outs in a tight contest, Yaz came to the plate. Nana said, "*Pfff*... He never does anything."

What? I couldn't believe my ears. My hero, leading the league in batting, home-runs and RBIs, and Nana said he never did anything? Indignant, I started to lecture my grandmother on the amazing talents of the Red Sox's best player. She listened patiently (I told you I was her favorite) as I went on to extoll all his accomplishments, all while Yaz was working the pitcher to a full count. As I finished my righteous rant, he swung at a bad pitch and struck out to end the inning.

Nana never said a word, but her expression said it all, as with an exasperated sigh, she gave me the "I told you so" look.

Sometimes you just have to admit defeat, and some opinions will never change. What else could I say, except, "Yup, you're right, Nana!"

September of my junior year - Nana, my mother and father outside a friend's cottage. My mother knit the navy blue sweater my father is wearing, and also the zippered sweater I am wearing. My sweater was gold and black, the Nauset High School colors. She sewed my varsity letter "N" onto the sweater and I wore it proudly. She was a talented knitter and seamstress, and made hooked rugs from scratch. Nana also knit, but surprisingly, she had learned knitting from my mother.

In Memory of Mae T. Riley – 1882-1978 – 96 years young

Tom Kane Spins Another Dick Cochran Yarn

Tom Kane was a legend on the Lower Cape: teacher, Truro town official, musician and most notably, writer. He wrote a weekly column, *My Pamet by Town Father*, for 43 years, detailing life in Truro and the surrounding area. A few times my father made it into one of Tom's humorous anecdotes, such as this one written sometime after 1980 in the *Cape Codder* newspaper, most probably in the late spring when the Celtics were involved in another playoff series.

As we wait for the familiar voices of the Celtics, (Johnnie Most's hysterical, raucous baritone and Bob Cousy's cultured, New England nasal commentaries), we get to think about the late Dick Cochran, our good friend and advisor back in the days when we labored in the Temple of Learning in Wellfleet. Dick was a benevolent, loveable man, portly, prematurely white-haired, heavy of torso with friendly blue eyes and an easy grin.

Despite his middle-age spread, Dick still showed the spark of athletic ability he had possessed in his youth. A multi-letter man at Tufts University, Dick had starred in basketball. In later years when he entered the teaching profession, he had assumed the position of coaching his favorite sport. Ours paths met at the neighboring shellfishing town. But Dick had arrived in Wellfleet shortly after the salad days of the tiny school's athletic triumphs. The school population had shrunk, while other towns on the Cape had either burgeoned or consolidated with neighbor towns.

Rival municipalities had built big, modern facilities, including posh gyms and sophisticated equipment. Despite overwhelming odds, Dick managed to produce several teams at WHS that provided adequate competition for the power houses of the Cape – Provincetown, Orleans, Harwich, Chatham. When time allowed we'd drop in after classes and watch Dick putting his charges through their drills in the tiny multi-purpose room that served as gym and basketball court. There were many occasions when he could barely muster up enough to form two squads.

"Low tide this afternoon, kids goin' down the bay oysterin'." But he'd give the varsity (Charlie Taylor, Johnnie Rochicheau, the Mallory brothers, Bruce Morton), a bit of a pep talk, stuff the whistle in his mouth and blast them into action.

"Give and GO! Put some mustard on those passes! Don't dribble the ball so high, you might hit your own head! New sneakers for you, son, tread's gone, and you might skid right through the front door. Don't push the man you're guarding, we don't have the stage pads up yet, and we don't want any broken ribs."

On one occasion we heard him explaining the mysteries of the pivot to his team. "A wall of humans in front of you, zone defense, arms outstretched, and you can't find a free teammate to pass to. You have to penetrate, here's how. And here, Dick, showing signs of his former skills would glue his toe to an imaginary sport on the floor, swing his free leg in a ballet-like arc, and cut around his man.

"Don't drag your pivot foot!" he'd shout as the ball swished through the net. From the sidelines you could hear Honk Taylor, a burly, muscular apprentice shellfishman and sub on the team growl: I druther bury my elbow in a feller's ribs. He'd let me through."

In a bit of parting advice, Dick would tell the kids to practice. "My brother and I learned to pivot by placing objects in the middle of the kitchen floor when we washed the dishes. Many's the time I hustled a soup tureen past two kitchen chairs and a hat rack on the way to the sink. Never dropped a dish nor touched an opponent...."

Tom Kane captured the essence of my father's coaching and his stories. I remember Dad's relating, almost verbatim to Tom's version, his anecdote about pivoting while washing dishes.

So – How Good Was He?

Growing up I knew my father had played and coached basketball, and realized he had been good. However, I had no standard to judge him against. Certainly, some exaggeration on his part could be expected, I must admit I may have embellished a few of my deeds to my own kids, at least a little. He shared memories with me, but in a matter-of-fact and humble manner. It turns out I had no idea just how good he was until I did some research after his death. Here are some highlights:

At Medford High School, Dick and his brother, Arthur, were in the same grade, although Arthur was younger. Together they led the Medford team, to a state title one year and a loss in the state finals the next. Dick was the scrappy defender, ball-handler and playmaking guard, while Arthur was a high-scoring forward, and one of the first ambidextrous shooters in the sport.

At Tufts the brothers played together for one year, 1931-32, culminating in a 12-4 record. In a game against Springfield College, Dick's set shot from mid-court beat the buzzer and won the game, 24-23 (low scores in those days, no shot-clock or 3-pointers, and very few outside shooters). Arthur was so good that he made several All-America teams as an "honorable mention."

Dick was captain his senior year (1933-34), and led Tufts to an 11-3 record, with Arthur serving as Assistant Coach. Arthur later became Tufts' basketball coach until he joined the Navy in WWII.

My father filled in for him, and took over coaching Tufts for those two years, culminating in a trip to the NCAA tournament in 1945.

Dick Cochran at Tufts in 1932 (jumping in darker uniform)

His Tufts team didn't have a player taller than 6'2" but they went 14-3 against college opponents, while losing five games to military teams that were all comprised of former college stars. In the NCAA tournament the first game was against NYU and their 6'7" stand-out, future NBA and Hall of Fame player, Dolph Schayes. They lost by a respectable eleven points, and NYU went all the way to the finals. Then Tufts, in the Eastern Regional Consolation round, played Kentucky and its Hall of Fame coach, Adolph Rupp, once again losing, but by a competitive score.

Some have asked me why he didn't stay in coaching, but to me the answer is easy: he enjoyed a simpler life. He didn't want the travel and stress of coaching college basketball. He was very laid back, and in addition was subject to migraine headaches that would have been exacerbated by the noise, lights and madness of college basketball.

So, he was very comfortable coaching in Wellfleet with its meager pool of talent. He sometimes demonstrated a move, but mostly he was low key and encouraging. Some of the players thought they were really good, and he never discouraged them, but I could always tell by his silent look he was not impressed; he had seen and played against the best.

Measure Twice – Cut Once

"Ricky, go get me the ruler," said my father from the top of the ladder. I scurried into the house, grabbed a ruler off the small desk in the dining room, scooted back outside, and climbed several rungs of the ladder propped against the side of our house. My father twisted his generous bulk, reached down, handed me the louver, and grabbed the measuring stick.

Dick Cochran had finally decided to install louvers to ventilate the attic of our two-and-a-half bedroom ranch house at the top of Taylor Hill in Wellfleet, Cape Cod. My father should've been "handy." At Medford High School he had been in the general program and taken wood and metal shop vocational classes. After graduation in 1928, he had gone to work for his older brothers, who were butchers and operated a meat stall in the original Quincy Market in Boston.

After a year of lugging huge sides of beef for his brothers, Dick had felt "he was keeping a horse out of a job," and college became more appealing. Fortunately, he had an avenue to higher education. He'd been a star basketball player on the Medford High School state championship team, and his brother, Arthur, was the leading scorer for Tufts. Their coach was very interested to discover that Dick was available. First, though, he had to take some more academic courses, so Tufts arranged an athletic scholarship at

Bucksport Seminary, a small prep school in Ellsworth, Maine, near Bar Harbor. It was late in the year, and the only scholarship available was for football (not his favorite sport), but Dick spent a year going through the motions of playing football, exceling in basketball, and freezing through a brutal Maine winter.

The next year he in enrolled at Tufts, where he became captain of the basketball team before graduating in 1934 with a degree in Civil Engineering. In the midst of the Great Depression there were few jobs, but there was always a place for a Civil Engineer. His first job was in Washington, D.C., working for the National Coastal Geodetic Survey, a job linked to his playing for the company's amateur basketball team. Within a year he was back in Medford, working for the city doing surveying for roads and sidewalks—which he found dull and uninspiring. He earned a teaching degree by taking night courses at Boston University and in 1937, with a young family, he found himself teaching math and science at Provincetown High School on Cape Cod. The next year he was hired as the teaching principal of the newly built Wellfleet Consolidated School, where he taught math, science, manual arts (shop) and boys' hygiene, and coached basketball.

All of his training was ample qualification to teach the manual arts. At home he had a mismatched collection of ancient hand tools, accumulated over the years: hammers, saws, a planer, an awl, a hand drill and bits, files, chisels, a crow bar, pliers, screwdrivers, a broken retractable tape measure missing its first half inch, and a rather unique 15-inch ruler. As a young boy, I occasionally eyed the motley collection of aged tools while my father gave me a lecture on the purpose, origin and history of each device.

For all his training, my father was *not* handy. Perhaps it was because he didn't particularly enjoy the tasks, or maybe because he tried to cut corners and never spent money on items that would have finished the job properly. In contrast to our neighbor, Chester Connors, a retired Industrial Arts teacher, my father was like an early pioneer, making due with the limited materials on hand. His occasional forays into home repairs ended with modest results and general disappointment.

Chester had built his own house, and his immaculate garage housed every hand and electric tool known to man. If you needed a tool or expert advice, Chet was your guy. Of course, this meant my father had to "stoop" to ask his good friend for help.

When my mother climbed the pull-down stairway to the unfinished attic on a brutally hot summer day, it marked the end of years of procrastination. Searching for some item that had been shoved away in the multitude of boxes, she spent way too long in the steamy attic. Sweating profusely, her patience exhausted, she delivered an ultimatum to her spouse.

Dad explained what was needed for the job. It involved buying two louvered vents for each end of the house. The louvers would let air circulate, but their design would prevent rain from leaking in. So off we went to Nickerson Lumber and, after the prerequisite chit-chat and catching up on the latest news, returned with two 12-inch-square vents, along with the necessary screws for installation.

Next was a trip to Chester's garage. I was big enough at ten years old to carry one end of the aluminum ladder. On a second trip we returned with a long, heavy-duty, extension cord and the electric saw required to cut the holes. My father propped the ladder against the driveway end of the house and adjusted it to the correct height. He flipped the electrical cord through the open bedroom window, and I ran into the house and plugged it into the socket. A pencil stuck behind his ear and a louver in his hand, he climbed the bouncy ladder with trepidation, hooking the electric saw to one of the rungs for later use. Reaching the top he realized his mistake. His plan had been to use the louver to measure and mark the size the hole. However, the louver's protective edges reached beyond the inner opening, in order to provide an outer seal to keep out the elements. That was when he called for me to get the ruler.

"So Ricky, these louvers are a perfect 12-inch square, and a ruler is twelve inches long, so I just measure one ruler-length on the sides and one ruler-length on the top and bottom. Now remember, double check your measurements. The old saying is: *measure twice, cut once.*"

With that advice, my father marked the opening, picked up the electric saw, and started cutting into the weather-beaten shingles, right through the wall. As the saw hummed and dust drifted down, something nagged at the back of my brain. I couldn't put a name to it, but somewhere in my father's monologue a word didn't seem right. What was I trying to remember?

Carefully, Dad finished cutting the opening, I could tell he was nervous handling the power saw on the shaky ladder. He turned off the saw, hooked it back on the ladder rung, and paused to survey the hole in the side of the house. Then he reached down again.

"Ricky, pass me that louver."

I grabbed the square aluminum vent, climbed the ladder and reached his waiting fingers. My father held the louver, and after a triumphant pause, he set it into the opening. The aluminum square went into hole, and then the louver and my father's arms plunged through the abyss, straight into the attic.

What had gone wrong? Instantly, I realized what had been teasing my brain.

My father pulled his arms out of the attic chasm, "Ricky, let me see that ruler again."

Once again I climbed the rungs and handed him the wooden shaft, knowing full well what he would find. He held the *fifteen-inch ruler* up for inspection, and realizing the error, his shoulders sagged with defeat.

Well, with some (humiliating) help from Chester, the too-large opening was restored to its proper dimensions and the louver was set in place. The second louver, at the kitchen end of the house, never did get installed. My mother knew enough not to push the issue further.

Sometimes when I'm involved in a home-repair project, my father's words echo in my mind, "measure twice, cut once." But, now I know the truth: measuring twice isn't always enough.

My father was pretty good at craving the Thanksgiving turkey

My Paper Route - The Trailer Park – and Chipper

The summer before fourth grade, Jay Sherwin and I were in adjacent pine trees, yelling pirate taunts and waving home-made wooden swords at each other, when a stranger stopped in front of our driveway.

"Hi, I work for the *Cape Cod Standard Times*, and I'm looking for a paper boy."

That sounded like an interesting proposition, so I climbed down from my pirate-ship-tree and listened to the man's pitch. I was only nine, and technically too young, but I was tall for my age, and I think the man was getting desperate. We went inside to talk to my parents, who were skeptical, but finally relented.

I got a canvas bag with the newspaper's logo and a metal coin-change-maker that clipped to my belt. The man took me around the route that covered Hiller Ave. down to Chequesset Village, back to Kendrick Ave along the bay, stopping at all the summer cottages trying to sell the paper, and finished in the trailer park. It was a mix of regular subscribers and summer tourists.

I was not the best paper boy in history. One day I was in a hurry and raced around the route. At one point I thought I heard Mrs. Ormsby calling my name, but I forged on. When I got home my mother was waiting. The newspaper comes in two parts, the *New Bedford Standard* and the *Cape Cod Times*. The two sections were packed separately and it was the paper boy's job to put them together, which I'd neglected to do. I should've had a hint when I finished the route with more extra papers left over than usual. That day I did my paper route twice.

The trailer park is at the bottom of Taylor Hill, and it was my bus stop where I waited with my classmate Tommy Berrio and his brother Buddy. Over the years I had some friends whose fathers were in the Army and lived in the park. It was an interesting place to deliver the paper with nice people and some real characters. One day an elderly lady insisted that I listen to her recipe for turtle soup before I resumed the route. Still haven't made that dish yet.

On my paper route I was always accompanied by my beagle, Chipper. The runt of the litter, he was given to us by Link Anderson and he was my faithful pal. Every day when I took the school bus home, Chipper sat at the top of the hill waiting for the sound of the yellow vehicle. Once it came into view he took off down the dirt path in time to meet me at the bus door. When I went to Nauset and started playing after-school sports, poor Chipper still ran to the bus, but didn't find me, so he'd walk slowly back up the hill and plop down in his favorite spot by the door with a dejected sigh.

Cousins and Guests

The piercing sound of the town fire siren caught my attention first; then there was a burning smell, and finally the sight of black smoke rising behind the house across the street. David Weintraub came running up his dirt road. "There's a fire in the meadow," he yelled. I took up the cry, yelling "Fire" through the screen door into the kitchen. In a moment the yard was filled with people: my mother, aunt, nana, and my cousins and their boyfriends.

My Auntie Evelyn, along with my cousins and the older girls' boyfriends, were visiting from Medford. Auntie and most of her nine children were just there for the day, but Donnie and Debbie were staying, while Peter and Tommy were heading home after their two-week visit. It was a mutually beneficial arrangement that gave my city cousins from a huge family a chance to spend vacation in Wellfleet, but also gave me playmates for the summer.

The chance to see a fire was too much of a lure, and following my lead the teenagers took off toward the Weintraub's. There we saw the flames of a large brush fire in the Mayo Creek meadow that ran behind the trailer park and below David's house. We went down the path to where the engines of the volunteer fire department had just arrived.

"Here, grab this," said one of volunteer firemen. "Follow me!"

We grabbed the thick fire hose and followed our leader as he moved toward the burning marsh grass with the nozzle set on a hard spray. More hoses filled the air with wet streams and the smoke turned from black to gray as the fire ran out of dry grass to feed the flames. Later, back at the house, our adrenaline was pumping as we laughed at our smoke-blackened faces and clothes.

My cousin Tom recently reminded me of this event. It was pretty exhilarating, and I can only imagine what it was like for my city cousins and their boyfriends. I don't think I could have arranged better entertainment for a bunch of teenagers. Most of the time my cousins spent at our house were far less exciting, but fun for both families.

My early years were like that of an only child, for better or worse, with pros and cons. I had two older sisters, but Judy was nine years older and my other sister Nancy was fifteen more than me. By the time I was old enough to remember her, Nancy was almost an adult, and soon had a family of her own. Judy was good to me, but in a big-sister way. Wellfleet was very lonely when we moved to Hiller Ave., and until Jay Sherwin moved in across the street I was pretty isolated.

My father was the ninth of ten children and I'm the youngest of the thirty or so paternal cousins. Except for my cousin Lynne, only a year older, I barely knew most of them. My mother only had one sister, however, Auntie made up for it because she had *nine children*.

Auntie, Uncle Dexter, Marsha, Billy, Gail, Lee, Donnie, Debbie, Peter, Tommy and Bonnie lived in tight quarters in a rented apartment, and so the trip to Wellfleet was a welcome break. The cousins who were old enough took turns staying with us. I remember Auntie always arrived with a box of assorted Dunkin' Donuts, a treat when Wellfleet didn't have the equivalent.

What my cousin Gail remembers most is sitting in our kitchen, at the built-in breakfast nook, listening to fairytales, Cinderella and Little Red Riding Hood, on our little portable record player. She delighted in having "alone time" without distraction from brothers and sisters. She also remembers our favorite playground, the sand dune behind our house and above Daniel's Packet Port cottages. All of the cousins were initiated into the thrill of jumping off the edge of the dune and rolling head-over-heels down the sandy slope, then hopping up and doing it all over again. Then we'd return to the house, where my mother and Nana made us brush off and shake out our clothes before we were allowed inside.

Of course, most people who live on the Cape find they have lots of friends and relatives in the summer. Funny how those folks don't visit in February. It's okay, we shared Wellfleet with a select few.

The fire alarm had specific meaning that was known by the volunteer fire department and most of the people in town. The signal code told the volunteers where to head to meet the fire engines.

Town of Wellfleet Fire Alarm signals
1 blast – 12 noon
        7:15 No school
        Fire all out signal
2 blasts – Center of town
3 blasts – South part of town
4 blasts – North part of town
5 blasts – Out of town – mutual assistance
6 blasts – Emergency Forest Fire

The Public Safety building with Police Station upstairs, across from the Town Pump with Duck Creek in the back – photo from "Wellfleet Remembered Vol. Four" by Ruth Rickmers

Photo by Warren Seyfert

My Other Father

After the death of my father in 1971, my mother sold our house and moved off Cape in 1972. That fall I got married and my wife and I established a new tradition of spending two weeks each summer in Wellfleet, sharing a cottage or rented house with my mother.

I lost my own father when I was 22, but I was fortunate to have my father-in-law, Milton Keane, for 42 years. My middle name is Milton, so perhaps it was fated that I would marry his daughter Ellen Keane; after all, how many Miltons are there in the world? I have so many "Milton Stories" they would fill their own book. However, I remember one that conveys his total confidence that he could do anything.

When Ellen and I were first married we rented a summer cottage in Wellfleet from the Sherwins that we shared with my mother. During our two-week stay, we were joined by a rotating group of friends and family, and most of the Keane clan. Tricia's husband, Donald, had an 11-foot "Kool" Styrofoam sailboat that he'd gotten by collecting cigarette wrappers (bizarre story, but true). The boat was a *Snark* class, but without the protective fiberglass outer shell, and only weighed thirty pounds. I referred to it as the floating coffee cup. On this particular day, Donald, an experienced sailor, and I took it out for a sail on Wellfleet Harbor in a brisk breeze. When we brought it close to shore, Milton waved us over.

"Let me take Susan out for a sail," he said, as we jumped out and Ellen's father and younger sister jumped in.

Donald asked, "Milton, do you know how to sail?"

Milton replied, "Donald, I'll have you know that I was in the Navy!"

I turned to Donald, "Milton was in the Navy, but he served on seaplanes. He has no idea how to sail."

But it was too late and off they went, the wind pushing them straight out and far into Wellfleet Harbor and Cape Cod Bay. We stood and watched the tiny sailboat disappear in the distance. Milton had caught the wind in his sail, but he had no idea how to "tack" or turn the boat, so they just sailed straight out.

Ad explaining how to get a Kool sailboat

In the late afternoon on Wellfleet Harbor, it's typical for the wind to drop off to a "dead calm," and just then, that's what it did. Suddenly there was no breeze, with Milton and Susan barely a speck on the horizon. Milton was always resourceful, so he took off the rudder and started paddling with it. The rest of us headed back to the cottage for dinner, while Donald and I took turns standing lookout on the beach, as the sun set and it turned dark.

In a "dead calm" it's also very silent, and voices carry over the water for miles. From the beach, you could hear Susan yelling, "Daddy, I can't believe you!" and Milton answering, "Come on, Susan, just keep paddling." Sometime, long after dinner, they made it back to the beach..

Milton Keane was a WWII Navy veteran, but it didn't mean he knew how to sail

Milton, a former golf pro, was far more capable at his favorite activity.

Summer People

Celebrities

Cape Cod has always been a summer destination for celebrities. Some appeared in productions at the theaters and music venues in Orleans, Dennis and Hyannis, and others simply used the low-key atmosphere and scenic beauty as a restful get-away from the show business grind. The lower Cape, particular Provincetown, going back to Eugene O'Neil, had a long history as a refuge for artists, writers, actors and intellectuals; the bourgeois set of the fifties.

Anthony Perkins

Wellfleet had its share of actors, writers and artists who sought an escape from the attention of fame. Wellfleet residents were intrigued by the influx of these famous people, but the reserved nature of the taciturn Cape native provided these summer visitors with the closest they could get to a degree of anonymity. Younger people will probably not recognize the names of the most regular Wellfleet guests, but Montgomery Clift (*From Here to Eternity*), Anthony "Tony" Perkins (*Psycho*), Eve Arden (TV's *Our Miss Brooks*) and Julie Harris were all big name actors. Henry Morgan, from TV game shows (*I've Got a Secret, What's My Line?*) rented a house at Chequesset Neck near my home on Taylor Hill, and

Montgomery Clift

Eve Arden

Henry Morgan

singer/actress Eartha Kitt (hit song *Santa Baby,* and her role as Catwoman on the *Batman* TV series) were annual summer residents. Erwin Canham was the editor of the highly respected *Christian Science Monitor* newspaper, and hosted a Boston-based news program, "Meet the Editors," a local version of today's "Meet the Press." World War II hero Admiral Chester Nimitz, who accepted the Japanese surrender, not only summered in Wellfleet, but was related to the Freemans, another of the oldest family names in town.

WELLFLEET PUBLIC MARKET
"Your Corner Grocery"
Corner Main Street & Holbrook Avenue
MEATS — POULTRY — GROCERIES
— LIVE PROVINCETOWN LOBSTERS —
DISTRIBUTOR FOR
S. S. Pierce Co.

Pen& Ink Wilfred Costa 1953

Wellfleet Public Market was owned by Vern Costa's parents, Wilfred and Harriet (Wiles) Costa. Vern was ten-years-old when Academy winner "Monty" Clift came in the store and spoke with him briefly as Vern was stocking shelves. Vern and his parents didn't know who he was, until one of their customers mentioned his name. I had a brief glimpse of him when I worked at Nelson's Market, and remember he had a receding hairline. Someone told me he wore a hairpiece for the movies.

Eartha Kitt-Catwoman

My sister, Judy, remembers Eartha Kitt shopping in Nelson's Market. It took Judy many days to get the nerve to ask for her autograph, and by the time she did, Judy learned that Ms. Kitt had already left for the season.

Julie Harris (5 Tony Awards, 3 Emmys, a Grammy, Academy Award Nominee, star of TV (*Knots Landing*) and cinema (*East of Eden, The Haunting*) was such a supporter of Wellfleet that the W.H.A.T (Wellfleet Harbor Actors Theater) has the "Julie Harris Stage" at its Route 6 location.

Writer and America's most noted literary critic, Edmund Wilson, was a year-round resident of Wellfleet, and his daughter, Helen Miranda Wilson, was my classmate in the early grades of Wellfleet Consolidated School.

Edmund Wilson

One of the world's most accomplished cellists, Bernard Greenhouse, summered off Summit Ave near our house on Taylor Hill. Famous artist Xavier Gonzalez and his wife, the noted artist Ethel Edwards, returned to their Bank Street home and studio every year. As a gift to Wellfleet, he produced a huge metalic sculpture of an angel that was mounted over the front entrances to the Town Hall. Sadly, the angel was destroyed in the 1960 fire that burned the building to the ground.

Ethel Edwards & Xavier Gonzalez

Xavier was a major supporter of the Wellfleet scholarship fund. Mark Sherwin of Wellfleet was a student of Gonzalez and was skilled at the silk screening process. Xavier painted

Wellfleet scenes each year that were then produced as a series of prints, to be sold for the benefit of the fund.

In the seventies, for several summers my wife and I rented a cottage at the Sherwin's Chequesset Village. On one of those stays, I got to watch as Mark turned one of Xavier's painting into silk-screened prints. We still have one of those hanging in our home.

That summer Mark invited us to the open house celebration of the print at Xavier's studio. I had seen him around Wellfleet for many years, but never met him personally. At the reception, surrounded by attractive people and pretty girls, Xavier came over to me, introduced himself, and gazed at my receding hairline, crooked teeth, broken nose and bearded face, "Your face has character, I'd like to sketch it sometime." He never did, but it was an interesting comment. I guess beauty is commonplace, but "character" is special, or at least I tell myself that.

Mark Sherwin's print of the Gonzalez painting-black & white photo of our gorgeous print -photo Rick Cochran

In the late sixties, the glamorous and sultry actress Faye Dunaway created a stir, when she took tennis lessons at the Chequessett Country Club. I'm sure I was not the only Wellfleet male who would've enjoyed watching Ms. Dunaway practice her serve in her short, white tennis skirt.

Taking a late-day swim at Gull Pond, Tom Murphy tried to convince me that we should track down the BeeGees, who were rumored to be renting in South Wellfleet. Tom had a vague idea of where they might be staying, and argued that although they were big rock stars with a hit record, they were still only teenagers just like us. It was an interesting argument, but I had to work as nightwatchman on the pier that evening, so we never got to meet the Brothers Gibb.

Over the years Wellfleet and the Outer Cape have become even more popular destinations for actors, writers, artists and celebrities. In recent years, rock guitarist Eric Clapton has moored his yacht in Wellfleet harbor; TV news and talk show hostess, Meredith Viera, is also a summer regular, as is commentator John Stoessel. TV actress, Debra Messing is a frequent guest. Actress Julia Stiles even has Wellfleet roots: her grandmother was a Newcomb, one of the oldest families in town, and her mother, Judy, owns the Newcomb Hollow Shop in the town center. Wellfleet Library schedules book readings by best-selling authors, and Payoment Theater in Truro (at the old Air Force radar base) attracts top performing acts.

"We'll Never Catch'em Now!"

Dr. Armstrong, Stew Jr. and Janet sailing the Valkyrie off Chequessett Yacht Club

"Dammit Daddy, we'll never catch them now," exclaimed Stew Armstrong, Jr., as the other boats drifted further away. His father, Dr. Stewart Armstrong, Sr., a noted vascular surgeon at Newton Wellesley Hospital, was skippering the family's "Lighting" class sailboat, the *Valkyrie,* in a race at the Chequessett Yacht Club in Wellfleet, around 1960.

At fourteen, Stew Jr.'s task was to second guess every decision his father made, as only a "know it all" teenage boy could do. My job was to "crew" which consisted of keeping my mouth shut, "hiking out" or leaning out over the side when, or if, we gained enough speed that the boat tipped on edge, and also nimbly jumping to the other side when the skipper yelled, "ready about," followed by "hard a lee." This meant we were "coming about," and the mainsail and boom would suddenly swing to the opposite side. I was quite adept at my limited tasks, but my best quality was keeping my mouth shut. After all, two skippers, a father and teenage son, were more than enough.

Stew Jr.'s frustration over his father's skippering was really irrelevant. The truth was we were never going to catch them, anyway. The good old *Valkyrie* was the oldest and heaviest boat in the Lightning class fleet. There was only one other wooden boat; all the rest had newer, lighter, fiberglass hulls. Even the most brilliant skipper couldn't make up for being the slowest boat in the race.

The fleet of "Lightnings" at Chequesset Yatch Club – photo Stewart Armstrong, Jr.

Eventually the *Valkyrie* became too old and leaky, so Dr. Armstrong replaced it with the new fiber glass *Isolde*. Suddenly the results changed, as the new boat propelled the skippers to racing success, even finishing 13th in the New England Regatta. Amazing what the right equipment can do.

Dr. Stewart & Robin Armstrong at Mayo Beach with water skies.

Stew with the Valkyrie and their dingy named Tristan. Yes, they were opera fans.

Stew's family became our July neighbors when Dr. Armstrong's dentist, Mr. Angus, insisted they use his cottage on Taylor Hill for free the first year. They loved the location, and it was a great break for me. Stew remembers playing on the sand dune, watching the Red Sox with Nana and me, viewing the July 4th fireworks from the second floor deck of their cottage, and drying out the soaking wet cotton sails by spreading them all over the furniture.

L-R In front of Angus Cottage, Captain's hats, Jay Sherwin, Ricky Cochran, Stew (top), little sailor, David, Janet and their lab, Sebastian (obviously too many captains) - middle photo- my dog, Chipper - Right phot - quahogin' with Stew at the Mayo Beach town bed

Stew introduced me to Gershwin's *Rhapsody in Blue* and *American in Paris*, and the Boston Symphony and Pops. He went on to become a high-school music director and then a school principal, something we have in common. We remain friends to this day.

The Weintraub Family

Down the dirt lane near our house lived David Weintraub's family. The Weintraubs came every summer from Manhattan, where father Eugene had a classical music publishing business. David and I were summer friends from about age six until our teenage years. He introduced me to Kurt Vonnegut, folk music and jazz, and was the only New York Yankee fan I could tolerate.

Russian born, Mr. Weintraub had studied violin and conducting at the famed Julliard School in New York City. Moving into music publishing, he had worked with Toscanini and Horowitz to arrange performances of works by Prokofiev and others, and had been instrumental in arranging the premiere of Shostakovich's Seventh Symphony, using a microfilm of the score that had been smuggled out of the war-torn Soviet Union. At Julliard, during the 1930s, he became friends with Bernard "Bernie" Greenhouse, who would one day become an internationally acclaimed cellist and founding member of the Beaux Arts Trio, considered the foremost piano trio in the world. In fact, it was thanks to Bernie and his wife Rory that the Weintraubs ended up in Wellfleet in 1951, eventually becoming their neighbors on Taylor Hill, just a short walk through the woods. One summer Bernie gave David and me a sailing lesson, and I found him extremely warm and patient.

Renowned cellist, Bernard Greenhouse – (Wikipedia)

Living in New York City, Mr. Weintraub had no use for an automobile, so his 1949 battleship-gray Packard sat in storage until the summer. Then David's father navigated the family from Manhattan to Cape Cod in a somewhat harrowing adventure, given a driver who only drove a few times each year. In Providence, Rhode Island, the family always stopped for a Chinese lunch, because Mr. Weintraub, a lover of shrimp with lobster sauce and barbecued pork, despaired of finding such delicacies during his three-month sojourn on the Cape. Arriving in Wellfleet the car was rarely moved. Mr. Weintraub preferred to walk whenever possible, highlighted by his morning stroll to Wellfleet Center to get his copy of the New York Times, and picking up mail twice daily from the post office, while leisurely visiting with whomever crossed his path.

David's mother, Lilien, was a sweet and gentle woman who loved gardening and birds. Well-thumbed field guides to plants, birds and animals were always ready at hand in the Weintraub house. As an only child, David and I shared a bond, since I was nine years younger than Judy, so almost one myself. We also shared a love for reading and baseball; David played first base on our 1961 championship Little League team.

Both the Armstrong and Weintraub families took me into their homes and treated me like a member of the family. My mother and father worked night-time summer jobs, while my elderly grandmother took care of me. So it was great to be able to go at night to the Wellfleet Drive-In with the Weintraubs, or play ping pong at David's or cards with Stew's family. During the day we played some form of baseball—catch, "pitcher-catcher" or "flies and grounders"—in the sandy lot across from my house. David, Stew, Jay Sherwin and I passed many hours refining our skills.

My first memory of David is when we were about five or six, and his family rented the Daniel house just below ours on Taylor Hill. We were getting blasted by one of the early 1950s hurricanes that shook Cape Cod. Wellfleet was so dead-center in the storm that the hurricane's "eye" passed right over us. During the dead-calm, we heard a knock on the door. David wanted to know if Ricky could come out and play. My father told the little boy to get home fast, because the storm was coming back. City-slickers, and without a radio, the Weintraubs hadn't realized it was only the eye of the storm.

David went on to Columbia University in New York City, where I visited him one weekend in 1969. We went to a "talent night" for local bands, complete with a psychedelic light show, at the then-famous *Bill Graham's Fillmore East.* David is the author of eight hiking and kayaking books about Cape Cod and the San Francisco Bay area, a professional photographer and a senior instructor in the School of Journalism and Mass Communications at the University of South Carolina. With his wife, Maggi Morehouse, the Borroughs Distinguished Professor of Southern History and

Culture at Coastal Carolina University, he still returns each summer to the family home on the back of Taylor Hill.

Story collaboration with David Weintraub

David's parents, Lil and "Sam" with their dog Golly and the old Packard, packed and ready for the drive back to NYC

Wellfleet Activities

Boy Scouts and Girl Scouts

Wellfleet had active Boy Scout and Girl Scout troops in the fifties and sixties. Like most boys I started as a Cub Scout and moved to Boy Scouts when I turned twelve. A high proportion of Wellfleet boys made it all the way to Eagle Scout, the highest rank in scouting, but I only stayed in a couple of years and never got past the First Class rank. I earned a few merit badges, marched in the town parades and generally had fun.

The Boy Scouts had a campground in the woods between Great Pond and Duck Pond. It's where I learned that you need to butter the pan when you fry eggs; I'm not sure I ever did get those eggs off the collapsible cooking-kit frying pan. The Legion Hall was our meeting location and Paul Daley, Mike Parlante Sr., Clarence Smith and Joe Pellegrino were some of our leaders. Paul had just returned from Air Force duty and recruited a number of men from North Truro Radar Station to help out. Before my time, Wilfred Costa, Charlie West and others had been scout leaders.

The summer I was thirteen I decided to try the Scouts' summer camp in Yarmouth, Camp Greenough. My friend, Jay Sherwin, had gone the previous season and loved it, so my parents agreed to a two-week session to give it a try. I had mixed emotions, colored by an event on the first day. All campers were required to take a swim test to determine their levels. Beginners had to stay in shallow water, and Intermediates could only swim in the enclosed area between the dock sections, but Swimmers could go over their heads, off the end of the dock and out to the floating raft that had a diving board.

I was a strong but unrefined swimmer, and the test seemed like a formality to me. A smug junior counselor, twirling his whistle and chatting with his buddies, told me to dive into the Intermediate area, so I performed a deep dive and held my breath to show off my endurance. When I finally came to the surface he told me to swim to the end of the area, do a turn and swim back, showing the strokes I knew. Well, I set off with a strong crawl, got to the end, and without touching the dock, turned around and swam back with an imitation of the side-stroke. I looked up with a smile, only to get handed a tag and told to take it to the waterfront director.

At the director's office I showed my tag, and was informed that I was an Intermediate. He then read a list of rules about my swimming limitations. None of it sunk in. Intermediate? I'd been swimming over my head for years, and nobody was going to tell me I had to stay in the limited area. So I did what any self-respecting, passive-aggressive, 13-year-old would do: for two weeks I never went swimming unless it was required. I sat on my bunk and pouted; guess I showed them!

Later I realized that I knew nothing about pool or dock swimming, and should have done a shallow dive and executed a turn that involved pushing off from the side of the dock. I was a salt- and open-water swimmer and didn't have a clue. When I returned home I finally admitted my flaws, signed up to take swimming lessons with my sister Judy, and got certified with the Swimmer classification.

Other than that, there were a lot of great kids and we had fun hiking, earning merit badges, and engaging in sports and other competitions. My table got in trouble when we made fun of the cook's rice pudding, and we were ordered to eat so many bowls that I thought I'd be sick. I had a problem looking at rice pudding for years afterward.

Overall, I enjoyed the two weeks, but not enough to want to stay longer. At the end of each session there was a "campfire" with a formal Indian-themed ceremony and parents invited. My parents came, and my always-practical father didn't think it made sense to drive back the next day to bring me home. So at the end of the ceremony he talked to the Camp Director and arranged for me to leave with them. This was not as easy as it sounded; I had to pack my stuff, then go to the waterfront to get my virtually unused Intermediate tag, go to the camp nurse and get some sort of paperwork, and turn it all into the Camp office,

So, stumbling in the dark with a dim flashlight, I set out on my tasks. I packed my stuff, finally found my tag, and headed to the Nurse's office. One of the few women at the camp, the young nurse had her own cabin that served as her office as well as her living quarters. When I got to the door, all the lights were out, and I really wanted to turn around and go back. However, I wasn't going home without the required medical paperwork, so, with some doubts, I knocked briskly on the screen door.

A moment later I heard voices and scuffling sounds. A timid voice called out, "Who is it?" I answered with the explanation that I was going home and the camp director said I needed some papers from her. I distinctly heard the sound of two voices whispering, one deeper than the other. Lights came on in the cabin, but it took a few more minutes, and then the sounds of shuffling feet from inside. Finally, the young, pretty nurse opened the door and let me inside, where I saw our handsome, athletic, head counselor sitting in a chair leafing through a magazine. Hmmm . . .

I didn't go back to Greenough, but it was mostly because I was missing out on the summer baseball season. Wellfleet had organized a Babe Ruth team and my time away at Scout camp had cut into my opportunities and passion for my favorite sport.

Scouts award banquet circa 1957 - rear L-R Wilfred Costa, Norman Gill, Charlie Silva - Front seated L-R Harriet Costa, Air Force Sgt, Barnstable Country Sheriff Tulloch, Andy Ramsdell

Far back next to and partially hidden by the coffee urn, Dick Cochran, - front back to the camera, my mother, Miriam Cochran and me, Ricky -across from me, Cliff Dalby – behind Cliff facing forward are Ray or David Rose and Mrs. Rose.

Eagle Scouts L-R Tommy Sousa, C.R. Lewis, Vern Costa, Andy Pierce circa - 1957

Andy Pierce receives his Eagle Scout badge from his parents, Leonard and Evelyn

Cub Scout Den Mothers—L-R - Gracie Francis, Katherine Dyer, Mrs. James Hooker, Barbara Horton, Myrtle Hopkins, Virginia Valli,, Peg Murray Dalby, Irene Berrio Pellegrino— Front right seated with merit sash, Dave Daniels

The girls had an equally active troop of Brownies and Girl Scouts, with dedicated leaders such as Estelle (Mac) Holt, Bertha Larsen, Jean Callis, Bea Berrio, Elaine "Trippy" Brown, Dottie Rose, Marty Smith and Mrs. Kasanovich from Truro.

L-R Bertha Larsen, Jean Callis, Estelle Holt- Girl Scout Leaders

Diane Silva remembers her first camping trip and crying all night because she had never slept away from home. Suzanne Grout remembers a week at Camp Greenough, where the girls were only allotted one week of the year, with the rest reserved for the Boy Scouts. Janet Holt, Jane Baker, Ruthann Rose, Sue Adams and Ginny Paine remember camp fires at Duck Creek, and Mrs. Callis' "hobo stew" and cooking "dough boys" on a stick over an open flame, trips to Edaville Railroad, and camping in Wellfleet and Truro.

Meetings were held at the Holt's Green Haven Cottages, and Janet remembers they used an empty cottage for sleep-overs. The girls remember the special ceremony when Mrs. Holt passed away. Girls Scout leaders in uniform formed an honor guard as a graveside tribute to their dedicated leader.

Wellfleet High School Activities

Class of '57 Junior Prom —Front L-R -Alfred Pickard, Norma Gill, Marcia Rose, Mary Moran, Judy Cochran (darker dress), Barbara Stewart, Gail Rowell, Susan Goodhue, Len Gates - Back L-R - Carol Daisy, Cynthia Hood, Joan Carey, Jim Hooker, Tom Hood, Mr. Kane

Wellfleet High School was a center for town activities, and not just for teens. Basketball games were prime entertainment in the dreary winter months. Wellfleet proms were attended by people from town, almost all of whom were alumni. Technically chaperones, the adults often outnumbered the students of the small high school.

Judy was President of her class all four years, an accomplishment only slightly dimmed by the fact that there were just twelve members in her grade. Judy vividly remembers her Junior Prom, because shortly before the event she got a bad case of poison sumac. My mother applied multiple layers of make-up to try to cover the rash on the face of her heartbroken daughter.

At the prom, while the Juniors danced, the orchestra leader scanned the dimly lit gymnasium floor to choose the Queen and her Court. At the dance's conclusion a drum roll preceded the announcement. The musician called out the members of the Court who came forward, and then finally the Queen: Judy. She went up to the conductor, who cringed as he saw her face up-close, and perhaps regretted his decision. Oh well . . . .

Another memorable event of 1956 was a large scale production (for Wellfleet) of the Gilbert & Sullivan play, *The Pirates of Penzance*. A creation that required the involvement of most of the tiny high school's students.

Girls front L-R Carol Daisy, Gail Rowell, Betsy Robicheau, Judy Cochran, ? – Standing L-R - Charley Taylor, John Robicheau, David Whiting,, Jim Hooker, Jimmy Townsend

Full Cast-Back L-R-Frankie Atwood, Bob Mallory, ?, Leone Hendrickson, Barbara Hanson, Susan Goodhue, Mary Moran, Joan Carey, Barbara Stewart, Cynthia Hood, Gail Rowell, Carol Yarborough, John Robicheau, Jean Carey, Marcia Lombard, Betsy Robicheau, Shirley Rose, Betty Paine, Judy Cochran, Marcia Rose, Connie Rego, June Gross, Miss Elisabeth Hooker, Music Teacher Stan Sorrento - Front kneeling L-R Bruce Morton, Carol Daisy, Jimmy Townsend, Charley Taylor in pirate hat, David Whiting in white, Jim Hooker, Ron Mallory, Ron Hooker, Jack Dillon, Marty Peters, John Daniels,?

A major event was the debut of *Hemo The Magnificent*, an educational TV movie produced by the Bell Telephone Company. The movie explained the blood-circulatory system, using the cartoon character *Hemo*. It was one of the first attempts at educational TV and was directed by the famous Frank Capra, who worked with Disney animators to appeal to a younger audience. In Wellfleet it was shown in conjunction with a Red Cross blood drive, with the whole school in the audience and local dignitaries in attendance.

Another significant production occurred when a Cape theater company performed the Broadway musical *Brigadoon* on the Wellfleet school stage.

Wellfleet Elementary Teachers
Mrs. Hilda Fleming

Mrs. Fleming

The Wellfleet Consolidated School, grades 1-12, didn't have kindergarten, which was not yet required by Massachusetts law. Fortunately for me, Hilda Baker Fleming had a private kindergarten in her home on route 6. Mrs. Fleming had been the first-grade teacher in Wellfleet since the 1930s, but had left the position when she married Bill Fleming, the Wellfleet Chief of Police. Her sister, Edith Atwood, had taken her place teaching first grade, and I was lucky to have had them both as my teachers.

Mrs. Fleming's Kindergarten 1953-54 —rear L-R Suzanne Grout, Karen Jones, Ricky Cochran, Jay Sherwin, Ruthann Rose- middle- Pam Murray, ??, front –Doris Crowell, Helen Wilson, Linda Blakely (sitting), Debbie Lombard, ??

Mrs. Edith Atwood

My family had many interactions with the Atwood family. In addition to all the information I told my wife in the first story, Henry Atwood was a realtor. After I graduated from Nauset, my parents ran the cottage-rental part of his real estate company during the spring and summer. My mother handled all the paperwork and my genial father drove people around to view their rental options.

Mrs. Atwood's First Grade 1954-55 - Bottom L-R- Tommy Murphy, Harriet Smith, Joe Francis, ??, Dave Eaton, Dana Murphy, Russel Murphy, Doris Crowell - 2nd row L-R -Pam Murry, Howard "Skip" Dickey, Karen Jones, Tom Berrio, Suzanne Grout, Jay Sherwin, Linda Blakely, ?? 3rd row L-R Ricky Cochran, Barbara Cole, ??, Helen Wilson, ?Jay Phelan?, Barbara Snow, Bobby Wilkinson, Debby Lombard – Top L-R – Albion "Buddy" Rich, Lynn Frazier

First-grade memories, maybe not so pleasant, include running up the cement steps on the south side of the school from recess, I tripped and landed flat on my nose—or rather, I landed on my nose, which then became flat. Dr. Callis said it was broken, but there wasn't much he could do about it anyway. To this day, I have an extra bump on the bridge of my nose as a reminder. Another time I was leaving the first-grade classroom and started choking on a hard candy. My father was there, and immediately picked me up, flipped me upside down, held me by my ankles, smacked me on the back, and the candy popped out. (The Heimlich hadn't been invented yet.)

The Atwoods and Flemings lived next door to each other, and Henry kept farm animals, most notably some donkeys that belonged to his neighbor. The highlight was the end-of-year field trip to the Atwood house, with every class member getting their picture taken with the burro.

Ricky - My mother had a thing for bow ties

Mrs. Adah Morton (Dickey)

Adah Morton (Dickey)

I first knew her as Mrs. Morton. She was hired in 1952 to start the new separate second grade, at a beginning salary of $2,500. Her son, Philip or Flip, was two years ahead of me, while her older son Bruce was in high school. Bruce was lively, energetic, athletic and the center of attention. He graduated with the last class from Wellfleet High School in 1959, and then went on to UMass-Amherst, where my sister was already a junior.

Despite his lack of experience, Bruce joined the UMass swimming/diving team. Practicing a dive, he got too close to the end of the board on his way down and gave his head a serious whack. Somebody needed to drive a frantic Adah to Amherst, an eight-hour round trip. My father stepped in to help. Whenever I see Bruce, he never fails to mention his gratitude for the show of friendship.

Mrs. Morton married Ed Dickey a few years after becoming a widow. The two were regulars on Sundays at the Congregational Church, where she played the organ and Ed graced the choir with his lovely tenor. Ed was a multi-talented man, skilled in the newest aspects of electronics, and an accomplished saxophonist and singer. He needed to pass the civil service exam for a job, and had to brush up on his math, so my father tutored him and he passed the test. I suspect the tutoring sessions were a half hour of math and a half hour of swapping stories, but it got the job done.

My father refused payment, but Ed wanted to do something in return. I was in fourth grade and intrigued with electronics (at least in theory), in particular the invention of the transistor radio. I saw an article in *Popular Mechanics*, "How to Build Your Own Transistor Radio," and showed it to my father. I mean, how hard could it be, right? Ed overheard the conversation, looked at the circuit-board diagram and said, "I've got those parts, I'll help you build it."

What followed were several sessions in Ed's basement workshop, where I learned about transistors, resistors, tuners, circuits and how to solder wires together. It was a bit overwhelming, and Ed probably did more of the work than I did, but it got finished. Then the big moment came. We turned on the radio and . . . nothing! I flipped the tuning knob through the channels, trying to find the Cape Cod station located in Yarmouth, but still nothing, not even static. Ed tested the circuits, and somewhere in *Popular Mechanics'* circuit diagram, there was a flaw. Poor Ed, he took over; for a week, he replaced parts, re-soldered and re-wired, but it never worked.

A week or two later, he pulled into our yard with a gift for me: a "do it yourself," one-transistor radio kit that used an earplug instead of a speaker and required very little assembly. I put it together and found that at night I could pull in two of the Boston

AM radio stations, WBZ and WHDH (there was no FM yet). I was thrilled that WHDH carried all the Celtics and Red Sox games. I curled up in bed with my earplug in place, falling asleep to the gravel voice of Johnny Most narrating the Celtics' battles against their evil rivals the Knicks, Hawks, Warriors and Royals.

Mrs. Morton/Dickey was kind, caring, soft-spoken . . . and a great second-grade teacher. My early-grade teachers were all vital to my development. I was painfully shy and withdrawn at recess; frequently I didn't join the boys in my class when they organized games. Very tall for my age, I was sometimes the target of older but smaller boys, at our multi-grade recess. These boys discovered I had a short fuse when teased, and this turned into a great game—for them. They would tease or provoke me until I lost my cool, and then I blindly chased them all around the playground, determined to commit murder if I ever caught them, as they gleefully stayed out of my reach.

With the kindness, support and patience of my teachers, I outgrew my early social awkwardness. In a few years, sports, particularly baseball, would increase my confidence and enhance my standing with the boys in school.

Mrs. Mary Peters

Mary Peters replaced Mary Brown, who had retired after 49 years (1909-1951). Her husband, Joe Peters, was the teaching principal of the Truro Elementary School and their boys went to Wellfleet for high school. I remember their youngest son Marty, who graduated from the last class of Wellfleet High School in 1959, and was fortunate to make the acquaintance of his older brother, Larry Peters, before he passed away.

Mary Peters at her 93rd birthday

In third grade I had a tendency to daydream in my own little world. One day Mrs. Peters brought a magazine to my father and showed him the cover picture. It depicted a little, blonde-haired, blue-eyed, boy, building a tower by stacking crayons, like Lincoln Logs, on his school desk. Meanwhile, in the background his teacher stood with her arms folded, her eyes rolled toward the heavens in exasperation. "Remind you of anyone we know?" asked Mrs. Peters.

Larry told me a story about his Dad explaining to his boys that they should be proud of their heritage because the Portuguese were good at three things that began with an "F." (Mary never let her husband finish the list and this is a family book, so you'll have to ask me in person. Sorry!)

Don't Fool with Mrs. Snow

Joan Snow, new to the Wellfleet Consolidated School, was hired in 1955 as a response to the baby boom. For years Wellfleet had combined classes: Hilda Baker (Fleming) teaching grades 1 & 2, Mary Brown grades 3 & 4, Albert Bacon grades 5 & 6 and Martha Porch grades 7 & 8. However, starting with the class ahead of mine, each age group now had close to thirty children. So my father had to hire more teachers and separate the classes into individual grades.

Mrs. Snow was a good teacher, but boy, was she tough! We never had any teachers who were push-overs; however, Mrs. Snow set a new level as a taskmaster. Having said that, we learned a lot! We also learned cursive writing, using the Palmer Method, and she expected us to do dictation, writing out long paragraphs that she read to us. I still remember the writer's cramp.

I hope my classmates have forgiven me, because I was definitely Mrs. Snow's "teacher's pet." I couldn't help it . . . not my fault. Mrs. Snow lived in Provincetown, where her husband was a lawyer and selectman and one of the few Democrats on the lower Cape. Her son from a prior marriage was my age, and sometimes he came with her to school events or basketball games. We hit it off right away and had a good time together. Later we played against each other in the Provincetown Little League, where he was a terrific player. (I was pretty good myself, but he was better.)

Forty Years with Mr. Bacon

Albert Bacon started teaching in Wellfleet in 1919, and when we had him for fifth grade it was his final year. Mr. Bacon was another strict teacher, not afraid to wield his ruler or yardstick and issue a smack on the hand or rear end. In his final year, he was showing his age. There were times he assigned us long reading passages, and then dozed off behind his desk until a snore snapped him awake. His classroom control was so strong that not a single student dared to take advantage.

We now had recess on the upper field, not behind the school at the "little" kids' playground. We took advantage of our status and roamed beyond the field into the wooded area, where we played Cowboys and Indians or Army. When the bell rang we were far away, and we waited to see if Mr. Bacon appeared. Frequently, he took his time, and we gladly enjoyed the extra five or ten minutes.

Diane Silva-Salvador remembers fleeing from Mr. Bacon's wrath. Diane and her co-conspirator, David Francis, were a year behind me in school, and Mr. Bacon retired (lucky for them) before they would have had him in fifth grade. One day at recess, fourth graders Diane and David decided it would be funny to tease Mr. Bacon, who was supervising the outdoor games. On impulse they started chanting, "Bacon and Eggs! Bacon and Eggs!" Mr. Bacon approached with a fierce expression, and the mischievous imps realized their mistake. Diane says she took off for the woods and hid out. Eventually she made her way back to school, and was finally discovered hiding in her locker.

It might surprise you, but Mr. Bacon was one of my favorite teachers. He encouraged reading and geography, two of my preferred subjects. He was also a member of our church, and coincidentally is now buried in the gravesite next to my parents.

Young Albert Bacon in 1930 - photo Ruth Rickmers "Wellfleet Remembered"

Photo courtesy of Pamela Thomas.

Wellfleet Junior High School, Seventh and Eighth Grades, 1930.

Front row, left to right: Anne DeGroot, Lawrence Osterbanks, James Delory, Helen Freeman, Lucy Taylor, Edward Lombard, Clayton Gilliatt, Margaret Hancock.

Back row, left to right: Pamela Williams, Ann Kendall, Olive Higgins, Teacher Albert Bacon, Evelyn Peterson, Natalie Kendall, Pulsenia Rowell.

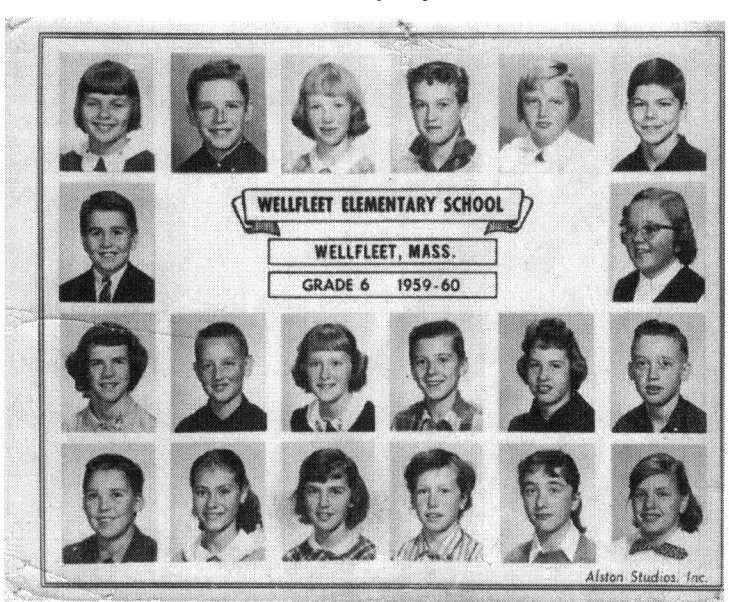

Mr. Harry Ryder

Top L-R -Dee ?, Howard "Skip" Dickey, Barbara Snow, Bobby Wilkinson, Lynn Frazier, Jack "GiGi" Ferreira-2nd row- Tom Berrio, Suzanne Grout- 3rd Down L-R - Harriet Smith, Rick Cochran, Janet Holt, Joe Francis, Pam Murray, Tom Murphy- Bottom L-R –John "Jay" Sherwin, Doris Crowell, Linda Blakely, Dana Murphy, ?. Maryann Buddensick

In 1959, grades seven through twelve moved to the new Nauset Regional and we were the first sixth grade at Wellfleet *Elementary* School. Mr. Bacon retired and Miss Porch moved from seventh-and-eighth grade to fifth grade/teaching principal, unfortunately depriving us of the opportunity of having her as our teacher. However, we had instead the entertaining and innovative teacher, Harry Ryder, an ordained minister and talented musician (playing several instruments) who also coached the last Wellfleet High boys' basketball team.

He excelled at creating learning games. We frequently reviewed geography, math and English by playing games like TV quiz shows, with teams based on our rows of seats. He even taught us the basics of classical music. He was infamous for playing practical jokes on students, but they were never mean or uncaring.

The sixth grade went to the cafeteria last, so rather than waste time, Mr. Ryder sent a scout to check how the line was progressing. One day he sent a girl named Dee, and told her not to come back until the line was short. As soon as she was out the door he said, "Quick, pick up your desks and follow me," as he opened our side door that went into the gym. We put our desks down on the gym floor and followed him back into the room to get our chairs. When poor Dee returned, the room was empty and her class had vanished. So, she went to find Miss Porch (who had been clued in to the prank). Miss Porch asked her a series of questions about the supposedly missing sixth-grade class, and stalled for time. Meanwhile, we returned our desks and chairs back to their places. When Dee and Miss Porch opened the door, Mr. Ryder was writing on the board as the class watched intently. Nothing seemed amiss.

"Mr. Ryder," Miss Porch said, "I heard your class had gone missing, but here you are."

With a wink, he replied, "I can't image what you're talking about Miss Porch," as we all giggled.

Of course, Dee was clued in before she doubted her sanity or became a strong believer in alien abductions.

We learned a lot and had a great time doing it. Years later, when I became a teacher, I often incorporated some of his teaching techniques, but never pulled off a classroom evacuation that included the furniture.

Miss Martha Porch – Old School Classic

I never had Miss Porch as a teacher, only as our principal when I was in sixth grade. However, she was so highly regarded I need to include her in this tribute. My sister and Cynthia Hood Cocivera have similar memories of the Wellfleet icon. Martha Porch was always "dressed to the nines": classic, elegant and immaculate. Her trademark was her silver bracelets, as many as twenty or more gracing each arm. Their musical chimes announced her arrival long before her appearance.

Martha Porch - Wellfleet legend

In an interview with Richard Fox for the *Cape Codder*, the retired Miss Porch imparted many pearls of wisdom that any aspiring teacher should take to heart. "I have always worn lots of bracelets. When I returned to a classroom where the children were waiting for me, I always took pains to rattle them as loud as possible. Sort of a warning, I guess, but they were all at attention when I entered the room."

Miss Porch was a staunch believer in *diagramming sentences* and her bracelets kept students' eyes riveted on the blackboard while she demonstrated the intricate pattern of noun, verb, subject, prepositional phrase, adjectives, adverbs and modifiers, as her arm produced a merry, metallic tune.

Miss Porch's pedagogical wisdom should be studied by education professors. I've used variations on this interesting technique when I taught.

"I had left the room to answer a phone call . . . when I returned the floor was covered with spitballs. I stood before the class (ignoring the mess) . . . asked them to get out their pads of scrap paper and their rulers. [I said] Now take your ruler, strip off four pieces... put them in your mouth, and get it wet, but not too wet. Now take it out, put it at the far end of your ruler. Now snap the ruler and send the spitball against the blackboard."

After the students had repeated the process several times, it looked like they had learned their lesson. Of course, then they had to clean the room. As a retired teacher, I now see the methodology of her techniques: jangling bracelets equals *it's far better to warn students you are coming so they stop unruly behavior, than it is to catch them in the act, and then have to waste time dealing with the disciplinary consequences.* Spitball technique equals *if you take away the fun and excitement from the student prank, it quickly loses its appeal.*

A highlight of the year was a 3-dimensional clay map of the United States. Students worked in groups creating the details of each region's topography, which culminated in merging the regions into one scale model of the (at that time) 48 states. Martha Porch lived on Commercial Street, never drove a car, and rode with students on the school bus to get to work.

Ron Stewart moved to Wellfleet in eighth grade and his favorite teacher of all-time was Miss Porch. Ron remembers watching the mysteries of sentence diagramming, something he admits he had never seen before and never mastered. When Ron was told that he had to repeat eighth grade, instead of being disappointed, he was thrilled that he got to have Miss Porch for another year. I guess I can't think of a better compliment for a teacher.

So those were my teachers, an eclectic lot with one thing in common: they all did a great job of teaching us reading, writing, math, geography, science and even music. We also learned manners, respect and proper behavior. I don't think we could have had a better background.

The Torch Is Passed

We all think are parents are immortal, sure everyone dies someday, but not your mother or your father, and certainly not at 63. My father died in his sleep during April school vacation of 1971, only six months short of his planned retirement. Tom Kane wrote a moving tribute in his *My Pamet* column.

"And on the other side of the Big Ledger, the shocking, saddening news of the death of our good friend, former boss and mentor at Wellfleet High School, Richard Cochran. Only a few days ago we had talked with Dick in the supermart at Wellfleet; mutually we had solved most of the problems of pedagogy, resolved the matter of long hair on teenagers, compromised our differences in taste relative to current music, inquired about each other's families, made a pact to retire from the grueling profession of teaching instander, bade each other Godspeed and good health...and now Dick is dead. He was a good man, an able teacher, a devoted father and husband, a gentle person. We consider it an honor to count him our friend. Ave atque vale, hail and farewell."

One of my father's best friends at Nauset Regional was the Latin teacher, Dr. S. Stewart Brooks, an Orleans and Nauset icon and the author of the column *Orleans Scenes* for the *Cape Codder* newspaper.

    "As we parted at the close of school on the last day before the spring vacation he said to me, "Have a good vacation." But now when I return to school for the final lap of the school's year I shall not see him to tell him that I did indeed have a good vacation. For last Saturday morning Dick Cochran died suddenly at his home in Wellfleet. I shall be the poorer for the loss of his companionship and our school will miss him as a teacher and a friend to all. I first met Dick back in the spring of 1943 when he was principal of Wellfleet High School and I was serving as head of Orleans High School for two years, while Al Leonardi was in the service. We attended many meetings together of the Cape Cod High School Principals Association, always in company of the longtime principal of Provincetown High School, one of the most congenial of all people I have ever known, George Leyden. Then with the establishment of Nauset Regional High School Dick transferred his education work from Wellfleet to Orleans as a teacher of mathematics. In the 12 years we have been together as fellow teachers at Nauset he became one of my closest friends. As Tom Kane, author of "My Pamet," has said on similar occasions, quoting the words of the Roman poet Catullus some two thousand years ago, on visiting his brother's tomb on return from a far journey, "Ave atque vale! Hail and farewell."

In one of life's cruel twists of fate, Dr. Brooks died less than two months later, on June 21st the last day of the school year. There is a faculty room in heaven, where Stewart Brooks, Tom Kane and my father are solving the ongoing issues of education and the world, while Elisabeth Hooker and Martha Porch chime in with sage comments and wise advice. To all the great people who taught me and decades of Wellfleet and Nauset students: Thank you, the torch has been passed, the lessons learned and conveyed to the next generations, your legacies inspire us all.

Photo Essays

The Old Pier and The New Marina	----------------	**117**
Mayo Beach and The Chequesset Inn	----------------	**123**
The Railroad Trestle and the Oyster Shacks	-------	**127**
4th of July and Special Events	----------------	**130**
Wellfleet Churches	------------------------------	**134**
Wellfleet Baseball	------------------------------	**137**
Wellfleet Consolidated School Classes	----------------	**139**
Miss Judy's Dance Studio	-----------------------	**160**

****

Fini --- **167**

The Old Pier and The New Marina

Until the early 1900s, Wellfleet had a number of wooden piers, but by World War II the only one that rema ined was the one that exists now. Located at the east end of Mayo Beach, at the junction of East Commercial and Kendrick Ave., it was a working fishing pier with limited docking resources. In the late fifties, Wellfleet harbor was transformed into what many called the finest harbor and marina on the lower Cape. The harbor was dredged to create a deep water channel, a breakwater for protection was built off Indian Neck, and the sand bar know as "Shirtail Point" was paved and reinforced with boulders to create an inner harbor with extensive docking for pleasure boats.

Many of the old Wellfleet Harbor landmarks were gone by the late fifties. Captain Higgins shack, often referred to as the "Spit and Chatter Club," was converted into a restaurant and moved off the water and across the road. Another landmark, the "lemon pie" cottages on Milton Hill behind the inner harbor, were damaged in a hurricane and replaced with conventional cottages. Their name was derived from their yellow paint and sharply pitched roofs that gave them the look of slices of lemon meringue pie. The "oyster shacks" on Duck Creek went out of use when the railroad stopped operations and gradually deteriorated into a favorite subject of painters, but by the 1960s even they were gone.

118

Early postcard Captain Higgins & Lemon Pies in twenties or thirties

Captain Higgins Spit and Chatter Club early fifties - Vern Costa

Captain Higgins - Lemon Pie Cottages in background – Vern Costa

Unloading, early fifties, notice no breakwater –Vern Costa

The pier before the marina-notice the lack of pavement-Vern Costa

Winter ice early fifties-there was just the wooden pier – Ron Stewart

Inner harbor in the 60s after the marina was built - lemon pie cottages were damaged in a storm and replaced with more conventional cottages -Vern Costa

Aerial View reminder of how our "narrow land" is a short distance between ocean and bay – taken after the marina project you can see the channel's slightly darker water, the pier and marina parking lot. -postcard

Aerial View before the marina, probably early fifties. Notice Shirt-tail point sandbar that was paved over to create the parking lot and provide extra berths.

Same view after the marina project.

Mayo Beach And The Old Chequesset Inn

The wharf and Inn abutted the small beach where we swam.

Post Cards of the era.

The Inn was below the future location of our house on Taylor Hill

View of the interior of the Chequesset Inn- postcard Suzanne Grout Thomas

Ice storm damage that doomed the Chequesset Inn – Suzanne Grout Thomas

125

The damage to Mercantile Wharf and the Chequesset Inn

Pier piling stub, all that is left of the old Inn. – Rick Cochran 2010

Historic marker, Keller's Corner, Kendrick Ave, Mayo Beach- Rick Cochran

Mayo Beach Lighthouse

Mayo Beach had a lighthouse located across from the recreation field - of interest to me is Taylor Hill in the background where our house was built in later years.

The lighthouse was moved, but the keeper's house remains. The lighthouse was recently discovered to have been relocated to Point Montara near San Francisco-Rick Cochran

The Railroad Trestle and the Oyster Shacks

Wellfleet's famous oysters made their way to Boston and New York City on the railroad. To expedite the process, oyster-shucking shacks were built on the side of the tracks where the trestle crossed Duck Creek. When the trains stopped running in the fifties the trestle and the shacks were abandoned and left to decay. The shacks were a magnetic draw for artists, intrigued by the slow decay and artistically challenging crooked lines of the old sheds.

When the tracks and trestle were still in place, but no longer used, I had a memorable experience. Jay Sherwin and I ended a day of play and "rambling" on the far side of Duck Creek. We could've walked down to Uncle Tim's bridge, but the railroad tracks beckoned. About halfway across there was a loud splashing in the water below. Glancing over the tracks we caught a glimpse of a large creature, clearly a shark, thrashing its tail in the tall swamp grass under the trestle. It was a thresher shark that stuns its prey with its tail, and then swoops in for the kill. Suddenly the trestle didn't feel very safe, as we thought about what would happen if we inexplicably fell in the water.

At home I faced a dilemma: I couldn't wait to tell my story, but, on the other hand, I knew my mother wouldn't have approved of us taking the short-cut. So I kept my mouth shut.

Postcard views of the Oyster Shacks on Duck Creek built alongside the railroad tracks. Trains stopped on the trestle and loaded the fresh shellfish for delivery to Boston and New York City.

Artists loved to paint the decrepit oyster shacks and abandoned fishing boats. This was the railroad depot until the fifties.- postcards

4th of July

Wellfleet loves to celebrate the 4th of July, and the summer holiday allows townies and summer folks to share the occasion. In the fifties Wellfleet started the holiday with a huge bonfire lit on fire at midnight to start the special day. The old bonfires were spectacular, but today they would be illegal. A tower was built by stacking old railroad ties from the abandoned train tracks. Stacked six stories high, the hollow middle was filled with rubber tires. Yes, rubber tires! The *piece de resistance* was an outhouse placed on top like an unappetizing cherry. Doused in gasoline, the creosote-treated railroad ties and rubber tires burned for hours, throwing thick black clouds across the bay and, no doubt, irrevocably destroying our environment.

Recreation activities (races, field events and games) were held on Mayo beach field, and, of course, the 4th of July parade was a chance for locals to indulge their often warped sense of humor. The festivities concluded with a spectacular display of fireworks. The first I remember were set off from Cannon Hill; we had a great view of them from the second floor deck of the Angus cottage, rented by our friends the Armstrongs. Later they were moved to Indian Neck, Mayo Beach and eventually shot off from a barge in the harbor.

Bonfire, Mayo Beach - July 3, 1956

Postcard provided by Suzanne Grout Thomas

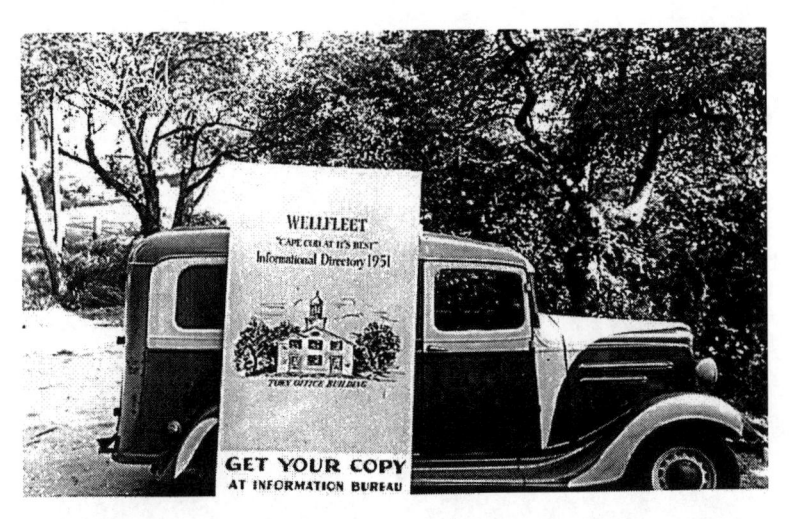

The Chamber of Commerce float advertises the 1951 brochure

Wellfleet Savings Bank Float with Doll Carriages- early fifties. The sign says "We have a Savings Acount, do you have one?" – think I see Pam Murray, Carol Larsen and Suzanne Baker – photo Suzanne Grout Thomas- her grandfather, Cyril Downs, was the bank's president.

Win Downs with only a barrel – Get your insurance from the Downs Agency – Suzanne Grout Thomas - early 1950s

Charlie Bean riding in the parade – photo Vern Costa 1964

Wellfleet Churches

Wellfleet churches are as beautiful and unique as any in New England. The old Congregational, Methodist and Catholic buildings were joined in the sixties by the modern-style Episcopal, St. James the Fisherman. Today the old Our Lady of Lourdes has become Preservation Hall and a much larger church is on route 6. Preservation Hall saves the beautiful details of the original and serves as an active community center. The newer church meets the size needs of the catholic community, because the original wasn't large enough, especially in the summer.

The Congregational Church is a landmark that can be seen by ships entering the harbor. Its majestic location provides panoramic vistas from its steeple. The church made *Ripley's Believe It or Not* for having the only church clock in the world to use the ship's bells method to chime the time. The clock was ingeniously designed by former Wellfleet selectman and craftsman, Laurence "Duffy" Gardinier.

Each church reflects the history of religious settlement in the region. The stately Congregational representative of the religion of the first pilgrim settlers. The Methodist, dating to the Methodist revival meetings held in tents off Campground road in Eastham in the early-1800s. Our Lady of Lourdes, meeting the needs to the growing catholic communities of Portuguese and French fishermen.

Congregational Church – postcard- perhaps 1960s

The original Our Lady of Lourdes ivy covered walls - postcard

Methodist Church - photo Rick Cochran 2010

St. James the Fisherman - postcard

Wellfleet Baseball

It wasn't until a decent field was built that Wellfleet had consistent organized baseball. The harbor dredging project of the late fifties provided landfill to create the field at Mayo Beach

1961 Little League - Champions of the Provincetown League - Coach Jim Casey on Left - Team members included Bill Galvin, Gene Casey, Johnny Wallace, Norm Pelligrino, Dean Paylor, Paul Francis, David Weintraub, Ernie Boutilier, Mike Ramsdell, Rose, Dale Smith, Ricky Cochran (the very tall guy in the middle) Team Record 16-1 including playoffs.

Pony League and Babe Ruth

Grainy Picture from a slide - Babe Ruth game - Len Gates umpire, Rick Cochran catcher, unidentified opposing team batter who looks like he's bunting – photo Vern Costa

A Pony League team started in 1960 coached by Paul Daley. In a few years the league changed from Pony League to Babe Ruth League coached by Vern Costa. Here are a few articles – funny how these clippings always seem to have me getting the key hit… afraid it didn't always happen that way. – Provincetown Advocate archives.

Pony League

Tuesday, July 21, the Wellfleet Pony League will play Eastham at Orleans, and on Thursday, July 23, they'll play the Orleans team at Orleans.

Players on the Wellfleet team are Bob Butterly, Bill Brooks, Bob Campbell, Gene Casey, Chris Clark, Rick Cochran, Jim Curran, Dave Eaton, Paul Hendrickson, Tom Murphy, Steve Philbrick, Mike Ramsdell, Dave Sarnoff, and John Wallace.

Pony League

The Wellfleet Braves of the Nauset Pony League nipped the Harwich team last week, 2 to 1. Dallas Wilbanks of Harwich pitched a no-hitter until the final inning when, Coach Vernon Costa reports, Rick Cochran hit a single to center field to provide the spark which led the Braves to victory. Wilbanks, plagued by wildness, walked in both runs, which enabled Wellfleet to win. Steve Philbrick of Wellfleet pitched a fine game, striking out nine

Braves Win One, Lose One

Coach Vernon Costa reports that the Wellfleet Braves Pony League Team coasted to an 11-1 victory over Provincetown last week. Wellfleet had a 4-1 lead going into the last of the 5th inning when they collected seven more runs. Rick Cochran, the Braves' catcher, hit a triple and a double to bat in five runs. Tom Murphy, John Wallace, Gene Casey, Mike Ramsdell, and Steve Philbrick also boosted their bat-

Wellfleet Consolidate School Classes

The new Wellfleet Consolidate School building on the hill opened in 1938, replacing the old high school building located near the Congregational Church. Dick Cochran joined a staff of long established teachers: Hilda Baker, grades 1&2 (1930s-1950), Mary Brown grades 3&4 (1909-1951, 49 years), Albert Bacon grades 5&6 (1916-1959, 42 years), Martha Porch grades 7&8 (1928-1968) and Carolyn Richardson (hired 1930), who taught high school business and commercial subjects and served as the assistant principal, and occasionally as acting principal.

To this strong group my father added the superb Elisabeth Hooker in 1942 (1942-1979) to teach English and foreign languages. Other terrific teachers were added over the years, including the irrepressible Tom Kane who could teach most any subject that was needed: science, social studies, French, Latin, you name it. An advantage in the tiny school was that students had the same teacher for multiple years. Larry Peters credited Elisabeth Hooker with the three college-bound graduates in 1950 getting into Columbia (Larry), Brown (Henry Atwood Jr.) and the U.S Naval Academy (Willis Rich).

I was fortunate to have some of these same teachers, but also other talented ones who were hired in the fifties to meet the demand of the increased enrollment caused by the baby boom.

140

Wellfleet Consolidated School - a Selection of Classes
Future WHS Classes of 1951 & 1952

First/Second Grade with my sister Nancy (top row right)

Mrs. Hilda Baker (Fleming) grades 1 & 2 – 1941

Bottom L-R –David Curran, Peggy Pickard, Maurice ?, ? Souza, Tony Austin, Clyde Smith
2nd L-R – Hazel Atwood, Nancy Atwood, Betty Pierce, Gene Howland
3es L-R –Joan Souza, Lois Valli, Ruth O'Connor, Barbara Taylor, Doris Berrio, Lilian Daly
4th L-R – Constance Dickinson, Ronnie Taylor (Thureson), Billy Berio, Nancy Cochran
Top – two pictures of Mrs. Fleming

Class of 1947

SENIORS

THOMAS BAKER
  "Tom"
  General Course
  Band 1,2,3,4.
  Senior Play 3,4.
  Baseball 4.
  Movie Operator 1,2,3,4.

VIRGINIA CASSIDY
  Commercial Course
  Sec. and Treas. 2
  Senior Play 4.
  Year Book 4.

DOROTHY HANLEY
  "Dot"
  Commercial Course
  Sec. and Treas. 1
  Senior Play 3,4.
  Year Book 4.

JOAN MURRAY
  "Joanie"
  General Course
  Basketball 1,2,3,4.
  Senior Play 3,4.
  Band & Orch. 1,2,3,4
  Cheer Leader 4.
  Year Book 4.
  Softball Manager 3.

JOSEPH PETERS
  "Pete"
  College Course
  Class Pres. 1,2.
  Student Council 4.
  Basketball Mgr. 3,4.
  Senior Play 3,4.
  Year Book 4.

FLOYD PICKARD
  "Pick"
  General Course
  Vice Pres. 3,4.
  Basketball 1,2,3,4.
  Captain of Team 4.
  Pres. Stud. Council
  Senior Play 3,4.
  Baseball 4.

LUCY RICH
College Course
Basketball 1,2,3,4.
Year Book 4.
Senior Play 3,4.
Mag. Drive Mgr. 4.

    RUTH SMITH
    "Ruthie"
    Commercial Course
    Senior Play 3,4.
    Cheer Leader 4.
    Librarian 3,4.

ADALINE TAYLOR
"Babe"
Commercial Course
Basketball
Year Book 4.
Senior Play 3,4.
Sec. and Treas. 4.

    BERNICE TAYLOR
    "Bunny"
    Basketball 1,2,3.
    Captain 4.
    Senior Play 4.
    Mag. Drive Capt. 4.
    Softball Mgr. 3.

ALTHEA MAKER
College Course
Class Pres. 3,4.
Basketball 3,4.
Band & Orch. 3,4.
Senior Play 3,4.
Year Book Editor 4.
Softball Mgr. 3.

    ERNEST TESSON
    "Ernie"
    General Course
    Basketball 4.
    Baseball 4.
    Year Book 4.
    Senior Play 4.

Class of 1948

IRENE ALBERTA BAKER
"BAKER"

"A daughter of the gods, divinely tall and most divinely fair."

This tallest member of the class is also the quietest. You'd hardly know she was there, except for an occasional loud pop or snap. But don't worry . . . she's all there! Those gorgeous green eyes that look so dreamy don't miss a thing, and when she does come out with a comment it will be right to the point. Wait till the Hollywood talent scouts get around to Wellfleet. They don't know what's in store for them.

Commercial course; school play 4; vice president of her class 4; secretary-treasurer of her class 1; basketball assistant manager 4; year book staff 3, 4.

KATHERINE LOUISE DYER
"KITTY"

*"Her eyes as stars of twilight fair,
Like twilight's too her dusky hair,
But all things else about her drawn
From Maytime and the cheerful dawn;
A dancing shape, an image gay,
To haunt, to startle, and waylay."*

A flash of big brown eyes and dimples, an irresistible giggle—here comes Kitty, right after Irene, as usual. What a secretary she'll make; as nimble at the typewriter as on the basketball floor, an ornament any boss would be proud to have on his knees!—what was that crack, Kitty? Another of your jokes, or your favorite brand of gum?

Commercial course; school play 4; basketball team 1, 2, 3, 4; orchestra 1, 2, 3, 4 band 1, 2, 3, 4; yearbook staff 3, 4; cheer leader 4; class treasurer 3, 4.

MARGARET REED TAYLOR
"MARG"

"Such a wise little mother!"

Any one in trouble will find a sympathetic heart and a helping hand from Margaret Taylor. Are you a new-comer? Margaret will show you where to put your books and find yourself a desk. Been absent? Margaret will hear you say your vocabularies, dictate your shorthand, and show you where the history references are. The seniors have voted her the Class Mother. We'd change that—she's mother to the whole school!

Commercial course; basketball manager 4; student council 1; president of her class 1, 2, 3, 4; glee club 3; yearbook staff, manager 4; school play 4.

ADELE WILES
"DELL"

"The true, strong, and sound mind is the mind that can embrace equally great things and small."

An excellent mathematician, Adele can usually give the right answer . . . to almost everything. Yet she is like a clam when it comes to keeping a secret, a trait that comes in handy at times. She has a strong musical tendency and a fine alto voice which renders her indispensable in her church choir and greatly in demand for our talent shows. We have never known Dell to be other than the finest of friends, always in a good humor, ready for fun.

College course; vice president of her class 3; secretary 3, 4; basketball 1, 2, 3, 4; student council 4; orchestra 1, 2, 3, 4; glee club 3; school play 4; baton twirler 1, 2, 3, 4; librarian 4; yearbook staff 3, 4; cheer leader 3, 4.

BURNHAM RICHARDSON GROSS
"Burnie"

"In arguing too the parson owned his skill,
For, even though vanquished, he could argue still;
While words of learned length and thunderous sound
Amazed the gazing rustics ranged around;
And still they gazed, and still the wonder grew,
That one small head could carry all he knew."

If it wasn't for this dear, dear boy we frankly don't know what the senior class would do. Burnham may arrive bringing up the rear, but he always brings it, anyway. He's not very big, and seems like the quiet kind. Why is it that there's usually a loud noise whenever he appears? If he isn't on the scene of something unusual, don't worry: he either knows all about it before it happens, or he soon will!

General course; basketball 3, 4; glee club 3; baseball 3, 4; school play 4; yearbook staff 3, 4.

GERALD RUAN PETERS
"Gerry"

"I am not only witty in myself, but the cause that wit is in others."

What a fellow this old Gerry Pete is! A student and a scholar, a good bookkeeper, the center of any crowd where the gang gathers and the noise is loudest, a ladies' man, a natural-born ball player, and the school's star actor. There's just one question that has us puzzled: why isn't he out on the basketball court instead of up on the platform behind the clock? Is he afraid to show his legs?

College course; student council 3; class secretary 2; baseball team 3, 4; school play 2, 3, 4; assistant basketball manager 3; yearbook staff 4.

LAWRENCE WALDO TAYLOR
"Capt'n Hawk"

"... Life, liberty, and the pursuit of happiness!"

Larry, otherwise known as "Capt'n Hawk", crams a good deal into every twenty-four hours. To hear him talk about his work at the First National you would think that he sat in a swivel chair behind a desk and gave out orders. If you want to find him, though, go down into the cellar and hunt around among the freight.

After work Larry becomes the "Constant Lover". He gets into his car and takes off with a roar and a rattle. There's always a gang with him except when he takes (?) out. Where does the night go?

The next morning Larry has to fight his way out of bed. He comes to school with his eyes half open; but his grin is still all right, and he can get by on that. The first thing you know it's afternoon again and he's off for the First National. He just can't keep away from those heavy boxes of freight.

When you get right down to what matters, "Capt'n Hawk" is friends with every one. Who could want a better friend?

General course; class vice-president 3; student council 4; basketball 3, 4; school play 4; baseball 3, 4; yearbook staff 3, 4; magazine drive 4.

Class of 1949

DORIS PATRICIA CAREY
"A poet is born, not made."

This quiet and unassuming person has won the admiration of all her classmates by the originality and talent displayed in her composition. She's the kind that's conspicuous by her absence; there never are loud noises or feminine idiosyncrasies attached to her presence, but the Forty-Niners lose part of their charm when Pat's not around.

Possessing a keen sense of humor, Pat is greatly interested in people, whether in books or life. She had read or knows about almost any book you can mention; is somewhat of an authority on music (a Gershwin enthusiast); and has further displayed her versatility in typing, drama, and any of those affairs of a mysterious nature which occasionally enlightens our days.

General Course: Class secretary 3; class treasurer 4; student council 3; Scalloper literary editor 4; glee club 1, 2, 4.
Plans for the future: Writing
Favorite Saying: You ought to be shot.

JEAN ELIZABETH COLEMAN
"Her voice was ever soft, gentle, and low, an excellent thing in woman."

Who is Jack-of-all-trades in the Class of '49? The class red-head, of course. Do you need your budget typed, or a poster made, or have you any other typical trouble? If so ---go find Jean. She'll tell you about the latest thing in planes, or the best way to develop your own photos, or about some weird adventure...and the first thing you know her work will be done, and yours too. Somehow, too, the "troubles" seem to have been smoothed out. Is it because you know you always can count on Jean to help?

General Course: class treasurer 4; Scalloper picture editor 4; Scalloper typing editor 4; camera club 1, 2, H. H. S.; secretary and treasurer camera club 3, H. H. S. pre-drivers course H. H. S.; library service club H. H. S.; luncheon service club 3; H. H. S. glee club 4.
Plans for the future: Flying
Favorite Saying: What do you want?
I'll do it.

EMMA FRANCES FISHER
"For she is such a smart little craft,
Such a neat little, sweet, little craft,
Such a bright little---tight little,
Slight little...light little,
Trim little, slim little craft."

Quite a gal, this; confirmed man-hater? That is, if we are to believe all she says when French or English literature turns to the "tender passion," we'd think that all men are diabolic and loathsome creatures. But certain whisperings in the corridors, the demure expression when the topic of conversation turns to Greek, makes us sometimes wonder, sometimes almost sure, that she'll not always remain Miss Fisher.

College Course; class president 1; class secretary 3, 4; Scalloper 2, 3; Scalloper alumni editor 4; school play 3, 4; basketball 1, 2, 3, 4; cheerleader 2, 3, 4; glee club 2, 4.

Plans for the future: Nurse
Favorite Saying: I can't--I know I can't.

DONALD LINCOLN GROSS
"I'm very well acquainted too with matters mathematical, I understand equations, both the simple and quadratical, about binomial theorem, I'm teeming with a lot o'news, with many cheerful facts about the square of the hypotenuse."

The knowledge that Don can put away between 8:45 and 9:00 A. M. is nothing short of amazing. Despite his assurance that school nights he is always "at home," he seems to need every second of the precious 15 minutes. But when class time rolls around he knows the answers, and then some. Confidentially, where would a lot of us be without Don's help?

College Course; class vice-president 4; Scalloper editor-in-chief 4; school play 3, 4; basketball 2, 3, 4; baseball 1, 2, 3, 4; glee club 1, 2, 4.

Plans for the future: College
Favorite Saying: You don't know.

ANDREW LARSON JOHNSON
"Hail to thee, blithe spirit!"
Andrew is the school messenger-boy and ambassador-at-large. Everyone likes this character, even the teachers seem to enjoy his novel explanations of why his homework isn't done. Andy is famous for his jokes. Wherever there is a crowd, there you will him, surrounded by boys and girls, inventing a new story or hashing over an old one...It doesn't matter which; he can always get a laugh.
General Course: class secretary 1, 2, C. C. I.; president of athletic association 3, 4; Scalloper advertising manager 4; photographic staff 1, 2, C. C. I.-C. H. S.; school play 4; baseball 3; glee club 1, 2, 4, C. C. I.-C. C. H. S..
    Plans for the future: Accountant
    Favorite Saying: Who------------------ME?

HAROLD WALTER KEW
"................After the ball."
Whether it's a basketball, a baseball or just a ball, Harold will be after it, and with plenty "on the ball" too. Here's an athlete a carpenter, and the sort of a fellow you can always count on, through thick and thin. Give him a job to do, whether it's with tools or his pencil or his brawn, and it will be done right, and on time.
General Course: class president 1; class treasurer 3; Scalloper sports editor 4; School play 4; orchestra 1, 2, 3, 4; band 1, 2, 3, 4; basketball 1, 2, 3, 4; baseball 1, 2, 3, 4; glee club 4.
    Plans for the future: Navy
    Favorite Saying: Hi, there.

MARILYN AMELIA MAKER
"She is wise, if I can judge of her, and fair she is, if that mine eyes be true; and true she is, as she hath proved herself; and therefore, like herself, wise, fair and true, shall she be placed in my constant soul."

The prettiest girl in the Class of '49, is Marilyn, one of the Honor Roll's permanent ornaments, the class's only female musician, captain of both girls' basketball team and the cheerleaders, and...but read the list below.

Ming will leave a deep and pleasant impression on all her school mates; she'll long be remembered for her friendly spirit, her gentle humor, and her refreshing mind...not to mention those green eyes!

College Course: class president 2, 4; student council 2, 3, 4; Scalloper business manager 4; magazine 3, 4; school play 3, 4; basketball 1, 2, 3, 4; cheerleader 2, 3, 4; baton twirler 4; orchestra 1, 2, 3, 4; band 1, 2, 3, 4; glee club 2, 4.

Plans for the future: Beautician
Favorite Saying:Come on kids, let's go.

WALTER SENIOR WADE
"Rara Avis!"

Here we have a fine fellow, but what few lines can edequately depict him ? Walter Wade is the life of the party...even if there isn't a party going on. His unpredictable remarks will one time throw us into uncontrollable fits of mirth, and another time cause us to stop and think about their depth and logic.

Wally is the "Daddy" of the Senior Class; his word carries leaden weight. But he is also a man of action. He is no piker; at moments notice he will roll up his sleeves and pitch in.

General Course; class vice-president 4, T. A. S.; Scalloper assistant advertising manager; school play 2, 4,; basketball 1, 2, 3, T. A. S.; baseball 1, 2, 3, T. A. S; timekeeper 3, 4; band 1, glee club 2, 4.

Plans for the future: Dental Lab.
Favorite Saying: Let's use psychology.

Class of 1950 – with notes written to Burnie Gross

We'll be no strangers for the next ∞ years.
—Henry

HENRY ATWOOD

"Hyperion's curls, the front of Jove himself,
An eye like Mars, to threaten and command,
A station like the herald Mercury
New-lighted on a heaven-kissing hill;
A combination and a form indeed,
Where every god did seem to set his seal
To give the world assurance of a man."

What a man! "Creamy" has it all: beauty, brains, brawn. On the Honor Roll, the basketball court, the band stand, or the dance floor, he seems equally at home. He's a generous fellow, and popular with all his school mates. The girls call him shy; maybe he's just waiting for the right young lady to come along.

College Course; Basketball 1, 2, 3, 4; Baseball 1, 2, 3, 4; Vice-President 2, 4; Treasurer 3; Orchestra and Band 1, 2, 3, 4; Yearbook Staff 4; Class Play 4; Movie Operator 1, 2, 3, 4; Chorus 3, 4. Plans for the future: College.

Behave yourself buddy.
Flip

WARREN BERRIO

"As happy a man as any in the world, for the whole world seems to smile upon me."

Who's the jolliest, friendliest guy in the whole school? Who comes crashing into a quiet room wearing a flashy shirt whose colors shout even louder than he can, and with a broad grin for everyone? You wanna bet? Yes, it's "Flip," always around when you least expect him, (watch him in a basketball game!) teasing the girls, arguing his way out of a hot spot, or backing up his wackiest opinion with an offer to bet on it. What will we ever do without him? There's only one "Flip" in the world.

General Course; Basketball 1, 2, 3, 4; Baseball 1, 2, 3, 4; Chorus 1, 4; Yearbook Staff 4; School Play 4. Plans for the future: Chef.

Hope the navy is good to you
Eugene

EUGENE CORMIER

"Life's a pudding full of plums
Care's a canker that benumbs
Wherefore waste our elocution
On impossible solution?
Life's a pleasant institution
Let us take it as it comes."

It's the quiet young man you want to watch, whether in class, on the basketball floor, or on a date. "Gene" can be counted on in any situation, for the right answer, the lucky shot, or his own unique self-starting (?) chariot. Though he's been tooting in Band and Orchestra throughout his school career, you won't hear "Gene" blowing his own trumpet. Deeds speak for him . . . but he has a pretty good line ready for use when he needs it, too.

College Course; Basketball 1, 2, 3, 4; Baseball 2, 3, 4; School Play 4; Orchestra and Band 1, 2, 3, 4; Chorus 3, 4; Yearbook Staff 3, 4; Treasurer 4. Plans for the future: Navy.

Best of luck to a swell friend

MARJORIE EATON

"She is pretty to walk with
And witty to talk with
And pleasant, too, to think on."

Belle of the Ball at Junior Prom or Senior Reception, Marjorie is also a musician, a basketball player (till her appendix put her out on fouls), an Honor Roll student . . . and one of those women drivers you read about. We won't even try to say how many fences and trees she has moved. But you'd never believe it to see her sitting demurely in class or study hall, her eyes on her book and her whole mind on the business in hand. She's the best letter-writer a class ever had. You can count on "Marj" to do any job she tackles, with thoroughness and efficiency.

General Course; Student Council 1, 4; Basketball Team 1, 2, 3; School Play 2, 4; Orchestra and Band 1, 2, 3, 4; Chorus 2, 3, 4; Yearbook Staff 4; Class Secretary 1, 3; Class Treasurer 2. Plans for the future: Private Secretary.

Best Wishes Annabelle

ANNABELLE LEE

"Here's to our girl with the strawberry curl—
Let the band play on!"

Annabelle's flaming curls in no way indicate her temperature. Her favorite expression is, "It's always cold around here!" But her heart isn't cold. She has a word of greeting and a smile for everyone, and if you want a helping hand you can always count on Annabelle. She may groan over her books and shake her head over all her assignments, but we notice that her homework is always done, and before the last minute, too. In Band, Orchestra, Chorus, and cheering section, you'll find Annabelle supporting her school with vim, vigor, and voice.

General Course; School Play 2, 4; Orchestra and Band 1, 2, 3, 4; Chorus 2, 3, 4. Plans for the future: U. S. Service, WAAC.

To a swell buddy, "Larry '50"

LAWRENCE PETERS

"There is music even in beauty, and the silent note which Cupid strikes, far sweeter than the sound of an instrument; for there is music wherever there is harmony, order, or proportion; and thus far we may maintain the music of the spheres."

"Larry" is our candidate for the Hall of Fame; he's a student, and a musician who can hold us all spellbound. He can be as serious as a professor or as witty as your favorite comedian. That laugh of his sets a whole room off. What an imagination! And what an actor! Hamlet or Romeo, take your choice.

College Course; School Play 2, 3, 4; Basketball Manager 3; Chorus 3, 4; Orchestra and Band 1, 2, 3, 4; Yearbook Staff 4; Vice-President of the Class 1; President 2, 3; Student Council 2, 3; Secretary of Student Council 3. Plans for the future: Music.

WELLFLEET HIGH SCHOOL

My very best wishes for a successful life, Louise Rego

LOUISE REGO

"And ever against eating cares
Wrap me in soft Lydian airs
Married to immortal verse,
Such as the meeting soul may pierce
In notes with many a winding bout
Of linked sweetness long drawn out...
Untwisting all the chains that tie
The hidden soul of harmony."

This shy, dark-eyed damsel is happiest with her violin in her hands, but much more capable at a variety of jobs than her protests would let you believe. Chemistry and French call forth groans and excuses for late homework; maybe that's because she's such a conscientious girl. You can hardly hear her in class, but in Chorus the sopranos would be lost without her.

General Course; Orchestra and Band 1, 2, 3, 4; Chorus 1, 3, 4; Class Secretary 4; Yearbook Staff 4; Class Play 4; Girls' Basketball Assistant Manager 4. Plans for the future: Nursing and Music.

WILLIS RICH

"So on the tip of his subduing tongue
All kinds of arguments and question deep,
All replication prompt, and reason strong,
For his advantage still did wake and sleep;
To make the weeper laugh, the laugher weep,
He had the dialect and different skill,
Catching all passions in his craft of will."

"Willy" is the spark-plug of the Class of 1950. He stands out in any crowd, a star athlete, a good sport; with a quick smile for everyone, especially the ladies, and the ability to talk his way out of any difficult situation. Though he sets many a feminine heart a-flutter, "Willy" says that variety is the spice of life. But we notice that he still talks about his "Holy Cow!"

College Course; Student Council 1, 3, 4; Basketball Team 1, 2, 3, 4; Baseball 1, 2, 3, 4; School Play 4; Orchestra and Band 1, 2, 3, 4; Chorus 3, 4; Yearbook Staff 2, 4; Class President 4; Class Vice-President 3; President Student Council 4; Movie Operator 1, 2, 3, 4. Plans for the future: College.

Class of 1951

WILLIAM ADAMS

*"There is nothing—absolutely nothing—
half so much worth doing as simply messing about in boats, . . . or with boats . . .
in or out of 'em, it doesn't matter."*

"Bill" is the little guy—but important to his classmates. He's always in there doing his share and more too. He not only shows his abilities in the F. N. Stores and studies, but on the basketball court as well. His free time is spent riding around in his boat with his favorite companion. No girl need apply—Bill prefers his dog. At school his exploding laughter will set off a whole room, but "Bill" knows his place when it's time to get down to work.

General Course; Orchestra and Band 1, 2, 3, 4; Chorus 2, 3, 4; Basketball 2, 3, 4; Baseball 1, 2, 3, 4; Yearbook Staff 4; Class Play 4; Manual Training 1, 3, 4. Plans for the future: Navy.

DORIS BERRIO

"Cherchez la femme!"

She is the quiet one, but certainly gets around. Interested in all sports, Doris glides smoothly on a dance floor and is right on hand when anyone mentions basketball. Her appearance and manner, along with her sincere conversation, can win her the way to any boy's heart. Her school work is equally neat. In short, "Dottie" is an all around good scout.

Commercial Course; Basketball 1, 2, 3, 4; Vocal 2, 3, 4; Class Play 4; Yearbook Staff 4; Class Secretary 3, 4; Class Vice-President 2; Class Treasurer 1; Student Council 4. Plans for the future: Business College.

WILLIAM BERRIO

*"The books I read and the life I lead
Are sensible, sane, and wild;
I like calm hats and I don't wear spats;
But I want my neckties wild!"*

When you hear footsteps approaching about 9:15, you'll know it's "Bill", whose excuse is, "Couldn't get my car started." (He lives only about a 2-minute walk from here.) He is the quiet one in class who never hears the question because of the noise the others are making. When told to quiet down, he puts on an innocent look and says, "Who, me?"

General Course; Treasurer 2; Vice President 3; Basketball 4; Chorus 2, 3, 4; Class Play; Yearbook Staff; Manual Training 1, 2, 3, 4. Plans for the future: Undecided.

LILLIAN DALEY

*"—the gayest of all gay girls,
Long in one place she will not stay,
Back from your brow she strokes the curls,
Kisses you quick, and flies away."*

"Lill" is always at the center of something, whether it's a panic or a party. Those blond curls, dark eyes and that nimble tongue can get people all up in arms. But wait a minute—Want to hear a pin drop? Just look in on Grades 1 & 2 when Lillian is their substitute teacher. She has them completely under her spell.

General Course; Basketball 1, 3, 4; Class Treasurer 3, 4; Class Play 4; Yearbook Staff 4; Chorus 2, 3, 4; Baton 1, 2, 3, 4; Plans for the future: School Teacher.

RUTH O'CONNOR

"I can resist everything except temptation."

When the school loses "Ruthie", it loses its chief source of merriment. Many a study hall has been set off by that contagious giggle and "those" jokes. The endless supply of gum will certainly be missed. When it comes to basketball, "Ruthie" can really work and usually murders her opponents or the "refs." Unfortunately for the team, "Ruthie" couldn't play this year because of an operation. But cheer up, "Ruthie", there's always the alumni game and (so we're told) only one appendix.

Commercial Course; Basketball 1, 2, 3, 4; Vocal 2, 3, 4; Class Secretary 2; Yearbook Staff 4; Manager of Play 4; Orchestra 1; Baton 1, 2, 3, 4. Plans for the future: Physical Education Teacher.

BARBARA TAYLOR

"After the verb TO LOVE, TO HELP is the most beautiful verb in the world."

Who could that girl be that just went speeding by in the new Chevie? Why, it's "Barbs", out for her daily excursion. This is the same girl that played basketball until she became the doctor's best patient. She is a standout everywhere she goes: a permanent name on the honor roll, and class president. What else could she wish for?

General Course; Class President 4; Vice President 1; Student Council 1; Basketball 1; Manager 2; Chorus 2, 3, 4; School Play 4; Yearbook Staff 4; Treasurer of Student Council 3. Plans for the future: School Teacher.

RONALD TAYLOR

*"I am the hero of this tale of woe
I'm Romeo, Romeo;
I am that sadly susceptible male
I'm Romeo, Romeo."*

This temperamental guy is a star in basketball as well as with his friends. You can't miss him in any class room with that hair cut and terrible laugh. When you hear, "I have the floor," you can be sure "Ronnie" and his body tissues are somewhere around. He is a man who spends little time in idle chatter, but he can talk when he needs to—either into or out of a situation.

General Course; Basketball 1, 2, 3, 4; Baseball 2, 3; Class President 1, 2, 3; Student Council 1, 4. Plans for the future: Armed Service.

RUTH THOMPSON

*"She was our queen, our rose, our star;
And then she danced—O Heaven, her dancing!"*

This girl is noted for being one of the most "easy-to-look-at" girls in the Senior Class. That nice smile and those friendly brown eyes have won her many a friend. She may have the appearance of being very shy and quiet when you see her in class—but don't let that fool you. You'll know better when you see her at work, on the basketball court, or cheerleading—and what a sense of humor. Although she stews about her heavy assignments, just notice that she always makes the honor roll.

Commercial Course; Orchestra 3, 4; Cheerleader 2, 3; Basketball 1, 2, 3, 4; Play 4; Class Secretary 1; Class Vice President 4; Chorus 2, 3, 4; Yearbook Staff 4; Student Council 2; Student Council Secretary 3. Plans for the future: Teacher.

1951 - 1st & 2nd grades- the future Nauset classes of 1961&62

THE SCALLOPER — 1951

First Row, left to right: Janet Huntley, Lloyd Ellis, Eileen Berrio, Hilda Rego, Carol Ann Davis, Thomas Pellegrino, Lee Frazier, Leonizia Thimus. Second Row: Andy Pierce, Leslie Hayman, John Broughton, Robin Fox, Gene Valli, Robert Pittman, William McKay, John Rogers. Third Row: Mark Wiley, Moniz Rose, Brian Blakeley, Chandler Crowell, David Daniels, Charles Valli, Ronald Crowell, David Zackary, Mrs. Edith Atwood.

1st AND 2nd GRADES

OUT of all the lower grades I think that the First and Second are the most ambitious. Never a moment is lost or wasted. If it isn't school work that they are busying themselves with, it is something to their own enjoyment. But work or play they remain busy and above all, quiet.

Mrs. Atwood has done wonders teaching the Second grade how to add, using dollars and cents. She also is teaching both classes how to tell time, and how to enjoy reading books from their own private library in the back of the room.

Entering this room one may tell, by a quick glance around the room, what season it is. If it is Christmas time, the room will be filled with snowmen, Christmas trees, stars, and Madonnas. In the spring there are Easter Bunnies and the proper decorations to go with them. Then, of course, there are Indians and Pilgrims at Thanksgiving time.

Before the year is over, they will have scenes depicting the country of Holland. There will be such things as Dutch boys and girls, windmills and tulips. Not only are the seasons pictured around the room, but they are celebrated with parties. The parties usually consist of games, exchange of presents or valentines, and of course refreshments—Ice cream, cookies, and candy.

But wait, we must not forget the Rhythm Band in which this class takes part. In this band they learn to play drums, cymbals, sticks, bells and other instruments. Some day in the near future you will see all these little students in the High School Band. They can now be termed as budding musicians. The class is now practicing for the Annual Concert in the spring in which they participate.

Lillian Daley, '51

**1951 top picture 5th & 6th - future WHS classes of 1957 & '58
Bottom 3rd & 4th grades – future WHS 1959 & Nauset 1960**

THE SCALLOPER — 1951

First Row, left to right: Cythinia Hood, Katherine Taylor, Mary Moran, Elizabeth Collard, Joan Carey, Leonard Gates, James Begley, Diana Gates. Second Row: Mr. Albert Bacon, Teacher; Peter Rich, James Kew, Joan Davis, Brenda Dickey, Jacqueline Smith, Gail Rowell, John Daniels. Third Row: Fred Anderson, Norma Gill, Susan Goodhue, Kenneth Taylor, Sandra Kelley, Marquerite Davis, Charles Taylor Jr.

First Row, left to right: Victor Wixon, Sharon Murphy, Margo Bacon, Leonora Hall, June Gross, Betsy Robincheau, Carol Sullivan, Shelia Lussier, Judith Dickey, Janet Sullivan, Alicia Moran. Second Row: Charles Carey, Vernon Costa, Sally Taylor, Judith Crowell, Barbara Hansen, Shirley Rose, Betty Paine, Violet Offett, Winifred Baumgarten, Vincent Berrio, Frank Atwood. Third Row: Myron Taylor, Bruce Morton, Lawrence Bassett, Irving Broughton, Stewart Hill, Richard Blackburn, Richard Taylor, Richard Huntley, John Collard, Martin Peters, Roger Smith, Paul Becker, Mrs. Mary Brown.

Classes of '54, '55, & '56 in 9th, 8th, & 7th Grades (some '57)

First Row, left to right: Shirley Taylor, Dorothy Rose, Elaine Schuster, Marsha Rose, Joyce Harding, Jean Carey, Dorothy Gates, Judith Rose. Second Row: David Whiting, Marsha Lombard, Leone Hendrickson, Lucy Taylor, Nancy Gerald, Linda Delory, Marion Davis, Miss Martha Porch. Third Row: Ralph Berrio, William Taylor, Paul Daley, David Carlson, Winfield Rowell, Robert Long, Theodore Moran, Leroy Ryder, Thomas Hood.

First Row, left to right: Edson Bagley, Alton Atwood, Gene Howland, Paul Tesson, Charles Rose, Barbara C. Taylor. Second Row: Bertha Dauphinais, Florence Frazier, Dorothea Smith, Alice Murray, Ann Lussier, Miss Martha Porch, Class Adviser. Third Row: Donald Moran, Robert Taylor, Robert Rose, James Moran, Noel Fox.

Classes of 1952 & 1953 as Juniors & Sophomores in 1951

14   THE SCALLOPER — 1951

First Row, left to right: Hazel Atwood, Betty Pierce, Margaret Pickard. Second Row: Nancy Atwood, Anthony Peters, Anne Peters, Miss Carolyn Richardson, Class Adviser.

First Row, left to right: Norma Rose, Shirley White, Robert White, Ernest Rose, Edward Maker. Second Row: Brewster Fox, Beverly Taylor, Sally Coleman, Caroline Franklin, Fred Baker, Miss Elizabeth Hooker, Class Adviser. Third Row: Irving Brondson, Robert Hautanen, David Becker, Luke Faust, Robert Newton.

GRADUATION EXERCISES

JUNE 16, 1954

EIGHT O'CLOCK

W.H.S AUDITORIUM

CLASS ROLL

Theodore Bedell (In Absentia)

Noel Fox

James Moran

Robert Rose

Barbara Taylor

Robert Taylor

CLASS MOTTO

FESTINA LENTE
(Make Haste Slowly)

Class Flower .... WHITE CARNATION
Class Colors .... BLUE AND GOLD

PROGRAMME

PROCESSIONAL	Festival March Orchestra	Bergen
INVOCATION		Rev. Lynn Townsend
CLASS HISTORY		Barbara Taylor
ONE WORLD THE HALLS OF IVY	Chorus	O'Hara Knight
ADVICE TO THE JUNIORS		Robert Rose
ORIENTAL FANTASY	Orchestra	Wilson
CLASS WILL		James Moran Noel Fox
CLASS PROPHECY		Robert Taylor
PRESENTATION OF AWARDS		Mr. Richard Cochran, Principal
GUEST SPEAKER		Mr. Thomas Nassi
PRESENTATION OF DIPLOMAS		Mr. Edward Dickey Chairman of School Committee
STAR SPANGLED BANNER		Chorus Audience
BENEDICTION		Rev. Stephen Smith
RECESSIONAL	University March	Bergh

Wellfleet's Most Talented Basketball Team 1954

Tiny Wellfleet struggled to produce a winning team. However, the 1954 team produced wins against larger school teams such as Bourne. Three starters were selected for the Cape League All-Star team. Unfortunately, the next year, the basketball season had to be cancelled, because too many remaining players were ruled academically ineligible.

1953-54 - Front L-R David Whiting, Noel Fox, Tom Hood, John Robicheau, Bob "Tink" Taylor - Rear - L-R - Winfield Rowell, Paul Tesson, Ted Bedell, Gene Howland, Jim Moran – Howland, Bedell, and Taylor made the Cape League All-Star team.

Class of 1957

Class of 1957 - Top – Mary Moran, Joyce Harding, Mr. Kane, Joan Carey, Gail Rowell
Middle – Len Gates, Carol Daisy, Jim Hooker, Judy Cochran, Cynthia Hood, Marguerite Davis
Bottom – Jack Dillon, Tom Hood

Last Graduates of Wellfleet High School 1959

Vincent Berrio, Winnie Baumgarten, Shirley Rose, Connie Rego, Judy Dickey, Dick Huntley
Betty Jordan, Bruce Morton, Marty Peters, Betsy Robicheau, Mr. Ed O'Brien
Eddie Tibbetts, Carol Yarbrough, Donna Harrington, Betty Paine, Stuart Hill

Wellfleet Dance Studio with Miss Judy

My sister, Judy Cochran, taught dancing lessons and our mother handled all other aspects: renting the Legion Hall, organizing the lessons, sewing almost all the costumes, and planning the end-of-year recitals. Judy started teaching at the end of eighth grade, when the dance teacher, Mrs. Zimmerman, moved and recommended that Judy was capable of taking over. Judy taught classes from 1953 until she graduated from Wellfleet High School in 1957.

Judy Cochran   Front L-R Suzanne Baker –Carol Larsen   Paula Jean Lussier
Back L-R Sandy Atwood – Betsy Hayman

Cindy Rock   Patty Pierce–Judy Linskey   Judy Belanger

Barbara Hansen – Anne Pierce   Elaine Ellis

Judy Cochran

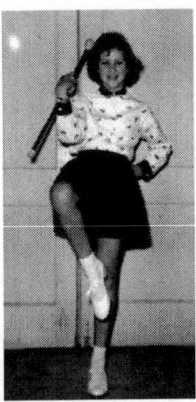

Stephanie Blakely

That's me, Ricky Cochran, looking like I want to escape, which reflected my general attitude toward dancing lessons.

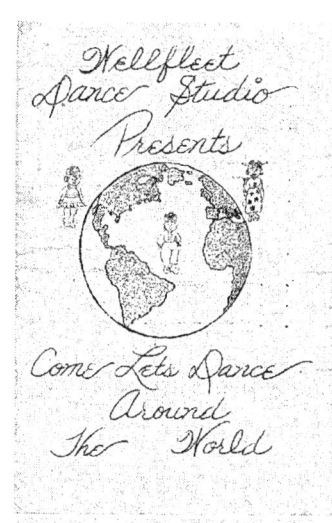

Wellfleet Dance Studio Presents

Come Lets Dance Around The World

COME LET'S DANCE AROUND THE WORLD

NARRATOR--------Norma Rose

1. SAILOR-----------Tom Doktor
2. AMERICAN HAYSEEDS-----Judith Belanger, Jane and Deborah North, Sharon Kimmel, Nancy Williams, & Barbara Cross.
3. SAMBA-------------Dorothy & George Kimmel.
4. THE FRENCH CAN-CAN---Betty Paine, June Gross, Gail Logan, Lee Frazier, Marcia Tinker, Barbara Hanson, Sharon Daniels.
5. VIENNESE BALLET-------Lou Woody & Paula Joan Lussier.
6. WALTZ---------------Elsie & Lloyd Rose.
7. IRISH JIG-----------Linda DeLory.
8. SCHOTTISCHE---------Suzanne Field, Marcia Rose, Marcia Lombard, Leone Hendrickson.
9. THE FOX TROT--------Tess & Arthur Daisy, Louise & Paul LaBrecque, Elsie & Lloyd Rose.

I-N-T-E-R-M-I-S-S-I-O-N

COME LET'S DANCE AROUND THE WORLD

10. HULA-----------Lou Woody & Paula Joan Lussier
11. RUMBA----------Louise & Paul LaBrecque
12. CHINESE TAP-------Betty Paine, June Gross, Gail Logan, Lee Frazier, Barbara Hanson, Sharon Daniels, Marcia Tinker.
13. DANCE OF MEXICO---Marcia Rose, Marcia Lombard, Shirley Taylor, Jimmey Begley, Joan Carey, George Logan, Larry Doktor, & John Tobicheau.
14. AMERICAN INDIAN---Linda DeLory
15. SWING-------------Betsy Tinker, & Tom Doktor
16. DUTCH------------Judy Belanger, Barbara Cross, Sharon Kimmel, Nancy Williams, Jane & Deborah North.
17. TANGO------------Dorothy & George Kimmel
18. POLISH-----------Barbara Hanson

FINAL-----------CORONATION

Queen---Lou Woody

Prince--Rickey Cochran

and the Cast

PIANIST----------------Leone Hendrickson

NOTE OF THANKS TO:

Props & Programs------George Kimmel
Costumes-------------Miriam Cochran

We wish to extend our thanks to both our families, our pianist, Narrator, pupils and their Mothers, who so willingly assisted to-ward the success of this Recital; also to the Towns-people for their help and interest.

Registrations will be accepted for Fall Classes

1953 Recital Program – Judy took over halfway through 8th grade year when the teacher's military husband was transferred. My mother organized the recital, sewed the costumes and handled the business.

FOUR-SEASON SWEETHEARTS

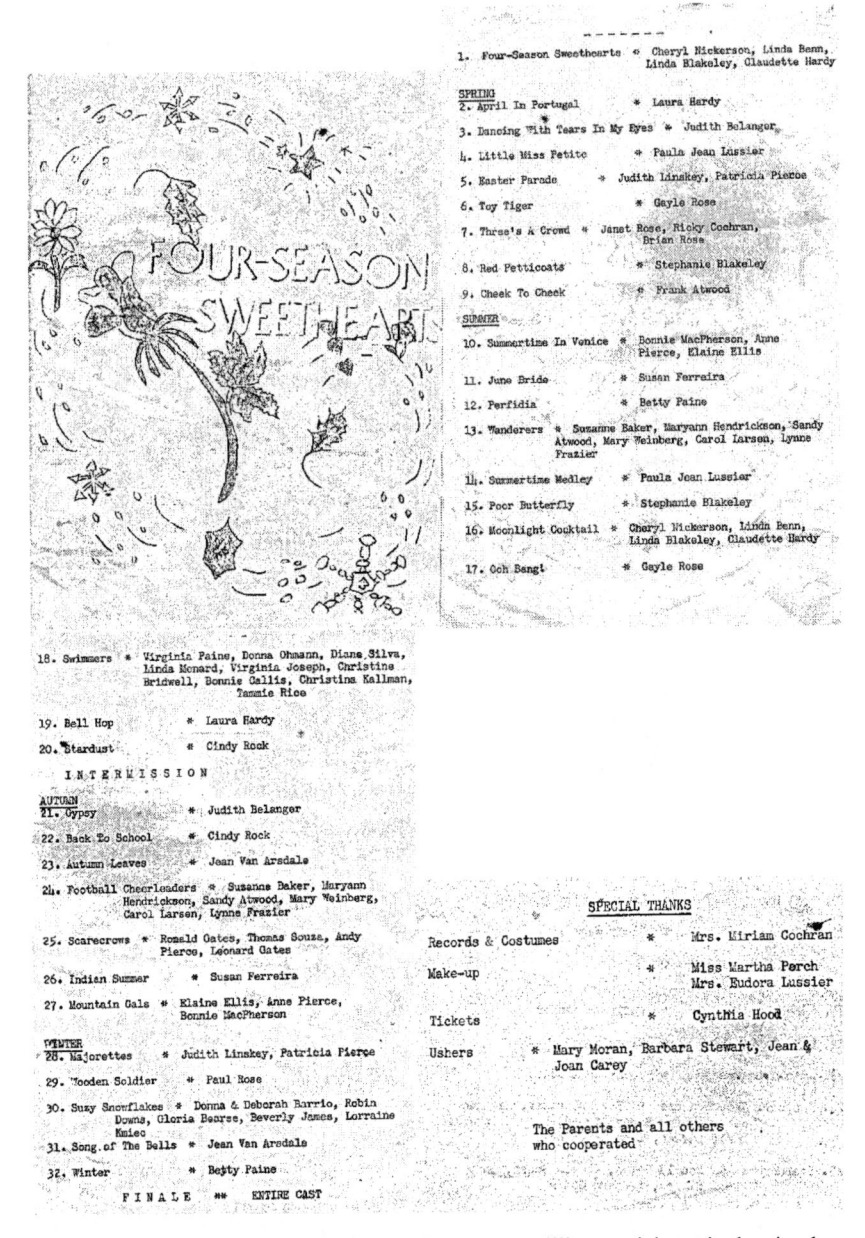

1. Four-Season Sweethearts * Cheryl Nickerson, Linda Benn, Linda Blakeley, Claudette Hardy

SPRING
2. April In Portugal * Laura Hardy
3. Dancing With Tears In My Eyes * Judith Belanger
4. Little Miss Petite * Paula Jean Lussier
5. Easter Parade * Judith Linskey, Patricia Pierce
6. Toy Tiger * Gayle Rose
7. Three's A Crowd * Janet Rose, Ricky Cochran, Brian Rose
8. Red Petticoats * Stephanie Blakeley
9. Cheek To Cheek * Frank Atwood

SUMMER
10. Summertime In Venice * Bonnie MacPherson, Anne Pierce, Elaine Ellis
11. June Bride * Susan Ferreira
12. Perfidia * Betty Paine
13. Wanderers * Suzanne Baker, Maryann Hendrickson, Sandy Atwood, Mary Weinberg, Carol Larsen, Lynne Frazier
14. Summertime Medley * Paula Jean Lussier
15. Poor Butterfly * Stephanie Blakeley
16. Moonlight Cocktail * Cheryl Nickerson, Linda Benn, Linda Blakeley, Claudette Hardy
17. Ooh Bang! * Gayle Rose

18. Swimmers * Virginia Paine, Donna Ohmann, Diane Silva, Linda Menard, Virginia Joseph, Christine Bridwell, Bonnie Callis, Christina Kallman, Tammie Rice
19. Bell Hop * Laura Hardy
20. Stardust * Cindy Rock

INTERMISSION

AUTUMN
21. Gypsy * Judith Belanger
22. Back To School * Cindy Rock
23. Autumn Leaves * Jean Van Aradale
24. Football Cheerleaders * Suzanne Baker, Maryann Hendrickson, Sandy Atwood, Mary Weinberg, Carol Larsen, Lynne Frazier
25. Scarecrows * Ronald Oates, Thomas Souza, Andy Pierce, Leonard Oates
26. Indian Summer * Susan Ferreira
27. Mountain Gals * Elaine Ellis, Anne Pierce, Bonnie MacPherson

WINTER
28. Majorettes * Judith Linskey, Patricia Pierce
29. Wooden Soldier * Paul Rose
30. Suzy Snowflakes * Donna & Deborah Barrio, Robin Downs, Gloria Bearse, Beverly James, Lorraine Kmiec
31. Song of The Bells * Jean Van Aradale
32. Winter * Betty Paine

FINALE ** ENTIRE CAST

SPECIAL THANKS

Records & Costumes * Mrs. Miriam Cochran
Make-up * Miss Martha Porch, Mrs. Eudora Lussier
Tickets * Cynthia Hood
Ushers * Mary Moran, Barbara Stewart, Jean & Joan Carey

The Parents and all others who cooperated

I believe this is the 1954 recital program. I was not a willing participant in dancing lessons, but with my sister teaching and my mother managing, I didn't have a choice.

PROGRAM

1. – Babes in Dreamland * * * Gayle & Paul Rose
2. – Rainbow Dolls * * * Linda Benn, Carol Blake, Linda Blakely, Suzanne Grout, Deborah Lombard, Pamela Murray, Cheryl Nickerson, Patricia Pierce, Cynthia Rock, and Janet Rose
3. – Spanish Tap * * * * * Judith Belanger
4. – Peter Pan * * * * * Paula Jean Lussier
5. – Soft Shoe & Waltz Clog * * * Frank Atwood and James Townsend
6. – Kewpie Dolls * * * Janet Blake, Christine Bridwell, Virginia Grodeckis, Jeanie Hopkins, and Kathleen Larrimore
7. – Arabian Dancer * * * * * Betty Paine
8. – Peasants * * * Stephanie Blakely, Laurie Cardinal, Elaine Ellis, Susan Ferreira, Elizabeth Hayman, Sheila Hill, Dorothy Huntley, Judith Linskey, Anne Pierce, and Helen Wilson
9. – Clown * * * * * * Sherburne Valli
10. – Top – Hatters * * * * Barbie Hansen & June Gross
11. – Rag Doll * * * * * * Judith Belanger

INTERMISSION

PROGRAM

12. – Country Girl * * * * Paula Jean Lussier
13. – Dutch Dolls * * * * Gayle & Paul Rose
14. – Boy & Girl Dolls * * * Stephanie Blakely, Laurie Cardinal, Elaine Ellis, Susan Ferreira, Elizabeth Hayman, Sheila Hill, Dorothy Huntley, Judith Linskey, Anne Pierce, and Helen Wilson
15. – Steppers' Tap * * * Frank Atwood & James Townsend
16. – Easter Bunnies * * * Janet Blake, Christine Bridwell, Virginia Grodeckis, Jeanie Hopkins, and Kathleen Larrimore
17. – Bowery Doll * * * * * Betty Paine
18. – Glad Rag Dolls * * * Linda Benn, Carol Blake, Linda Blakely, Suzanne Grout, Deborah Lombard, Pamela Murray, Cheryl Nickerson, Patricia Pierce, Cynthia Rock, and Janet Rose
19. – Little White Duck * * * * Paula Jean Lussier
20. – Flappers * * * * June Gross & Barbie Hansen
21. – Tillie's Tango * * * * Judy Cochran

FINALE * * * * *
Entire Cast

RECORDS & COSTUMES * * * * Mrs. Miriam Cochran
MAKE – UP * * * * * Miss Martha Perch
TICKETS * * * * Cynthia Hood
USHERS * * * Mary Moran, Carol Laisy, and Carol Ann Tiernan

Special thanks – to the mothers and all those who assisted.

REGISTRATION WILL BE ACCEPTED FOR FALL CLASSES

1955 Babes In Toyland program
Wellfleet Dance Studio just about broke even. The affordable tuition covered the rental of Legion Hall and the recital materials. Some years Judy had as many as sixty students and had to choreograph more than thirty routines.

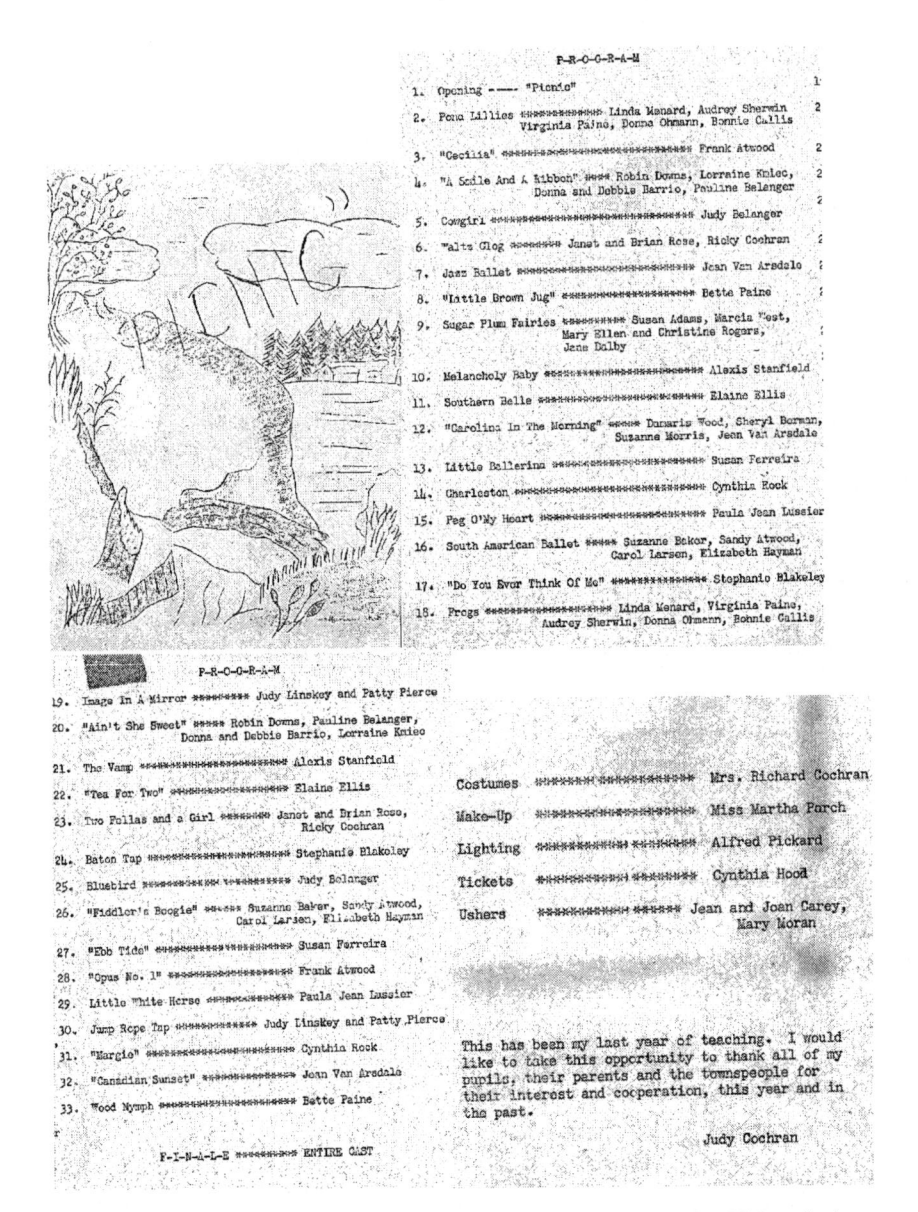

P-R-O-G-R-A-M

1. Opening ---- "Picnic"
2. Pond Lillies .... Linda Menard, Audrey Sherwin, Virginia Paine, Donna Ohmann, Bonnie Callis
3. "Cecilia" .... Frank Atwood
4. "A Smile And A Ribbon" .... Robin Downs, Lorraine Kniec, Donna and Debbie Barrio, Pauline Belanger
5. Cowgirl .... Judy Belanger
6. Waltz Clog .... Janet and Brian Rose, Ricky Cochran
7. Jazz Ballet .... Jean Van Arsdale
8. "Little Brown Jug" .... Bette Paine
9. Sugar Plum Fairies .... Susan Adams, Marcia West, Mary Ellen and Christine Rogers, Jane Dalby
10. Melancholy Baby .... Alexis Stanfield
11. Southern Belle .... Elaine Ellis
12. "Carolina In The Morning" ..... Damaris Wood, Sheryl Berman, Suzanne Morris, Jean Van Arsdale
13. Little Ballerina .... Susan Ferreira
14. Charleston .... Cynthia Rock
15. Peg O'My Heart .... Paula Jean Lussier
16. South American Ballet ..... Suzanne Baker, Sandy Atwood, Carol Larsen, Elizabeth Hayman
17. "Do You Ever Think Of Me" .... Stephanie Blakeley
18. Frogs .... Linda Menard, Virginia Paine, Audrey Sherwin, Donna Ohmann, Bonnie Callis

P-R-O-G-R-A-M

19. Image In A Mirror .... Judy Linskey and Patty Pierce
20. "Ain't She Sweet" ..... Robin Downs, Pauline Belanger, Donna and Debbie Barrio, Lorraine Kniec
21. The Vamp .... Alexis Stanfield
22. "Tea For Two" .... Elaine Ellis
23. Two Fellas and a Girl ...... Janet and Brian Rose, Ricky Cochran
24. Baton Tap .... Stephanie Blakeley
25. Bluebird .... Judy Belanger
26. "Fiddler's Boogie" ...... Suzanne Baker, Sandy Atwood, Carol Larsen, Elizabeth Hayman
27. "Ebb Tide" .... Susan Ferreira
28. "Opus No. 1" .... Frank Atwood
29. Little White Horse .... Paula Jean Lussier
30. Jump Rope Tap .... Judy Linskey and Patty Pierce
31. "Margie" .... Cynthia Rock
32. "Canadian Sunset" .... Jean Van Arsdale
33. Wood Nymph .... Bette Paine

F-I-N-A-L-E .... ENTIRE CAST

Costumes .... Mrs. Richard Cochran
Make-Up .... Miss Martha Porch
Lighting .... Alfred Pickard
Tickets .... Cynthia Hood
Ushers .... Jean and Joan Carey, Mary Moran

This has been my last year of teaching. I would like to take this opportunity to thank all of my pupils, their parents and the townspeople for their interest and cooperation, this year and in the past.

Judy Cochran

1957 the final year of Wellfleet Dance Studio. In the fall Judy started at UMass Amherst

Fini

At the conclusion of a movie, *The End* appears on the screen. Personally, I always liked the French word, *Fini,* which flashes on the screen at the close of their films. Fini is more than the end; it means: completed, finished. I like the subtle different.

In my books I often inscribed the phrase, "The times and people change, but Wellfleet endures." The message conveys that while my era in Wellfleet is complete, the memories continue. In fact, new generations of children create their own remembrances.

There is a catchphrase in literature and movies: "a coming of age piece." I suppose my stories fit that genre. When a friend read my tribute to Brian Ramsdell in my first book, he wrote, "I was in that car, riding around listening to the radio with my buddies; different car, different friends, different town, but I was there." I savor that compliment; it shows that people can relate to the stories, and match them with events in their own experience.

Memory is a funny thing. Our brain is like a wired circuit board. The memories are all in there, we just need the wires to make the connections. Sometimes a forgotten memory, sitting untouched for years, gets touched by the wire of the comment or conversation of a friend, perhaps even a story in a book. I find this happens to me, and I hope these stories and photos have rekindled pleasant, forgotten thoughts for you.

Made in the USA
Middletown, DE
31 May 2016